KINGDOM
LIVING

KINGDOM LIVING

JACK W. HAYFORD

Executive Editor

THOMAS NELSON
Since 1798

NASHVILLE DALLAS MEXICO CITY RIO DE JANEIRO BEIJING

Published in Nashville, Tennessee. Thomas Nelson is a trademark of Thomas Nelson, Inc.

Thomas Nelson, Inc. titles may be purchased in bulk for educational, business, fundraising, or sales promotional use. For information, please email SpecialMarkets@ThomasNelson.com.

Unless otherwise indicated, all Scripture quotations are from the New King James Version, copyright © 1979, 1980, 1982, 1990, 2004 by Thomas Nelson, Inc.

Hayford, Jack W.

Kingdom Living

ISBN 13: 978-1-4185-3327-4

Printed in the United States of America
HB 01.30.2024

TABLE OF CONTENTS

What is the Kingdom of God?

A KINGDOM IS A PLACE where a king rules. The kingdom of God is wherever God reigns through the lives of His people. And those who believe in Christ as Savior and Lord are God's beloved people. The kingdom of God is invisible because God is Spirit, therefore His kingdom is not visible to the natural. It is a spiritual kingdom. Jesus Christ said, "The kingdom of God is within you" (Luke 17:21). And when God lives through your life, He reigns in His kingdom.

In the Lord's Prayer, Jesus gave us a petition to God: "Your kingdom come. Your will be done on earth as *it is* in heaven" (Matthew 6:10). This prayer shows the priority Jesus gave to the kingdom of God. The kingdom of God will come on Earth when the will of God is enacted here as it is in heaven, when the visible world totally reflects God's invisible world. In the kingdom of God, everything yields to God's authority and power. All of His creation bows in perpetual obedience and adoration to Him. In the visible world, where satan rules, there is resistance to God's will. But God is relentlessly pursuing His kingdom! So what does it look like?

The kingdom of God is eternal. The kingdom is worship. The kingdom is His will. The kingdom is here unfolding in our midst. It is a kingdom in which we must see and learn to operate as citizens and servants of the King. Wherever there are those who honor Jesus Christ, the King, and wherever the Spirit of the King is, there is the kingdom of God.

As you work through this study, recognize that you are a citizen of an eternal kingdom. You are subject to its laws and privileged to receive all its benefits. Seize them. King Jesus is on His throne and whenever we serve Him, and wherever the Holy Spirit rules, there the kingdom of God is made manifest. And when God reigns, His glory and majesty is revealed in the earth. Let God arise . . .

Keys of the Kingdom

KEYS CAN BE SYMBOLS of possession of the right and ability to acquire, clarify, open or ignite. Keys can be concepts that unleash mind-boggling possibilities and opportunities. Keys clear the way to a possibility otherwise undiscovered or obstructed.

Jesus spoke of keys: "And I will give you the keys of the kingdom of heaven, and whatever you bind on earth will be bound in heaven, and whatever you loose on earth will be loosed in heaven" (Matthew 16:19).

While Jesus did not define the "keys" He has given, it is clear that He did confer specific tools upon His church which grant us access to a realm of spiritual "partnership" with Him. The "keys" are concepts or biblical themes, traceable throughout Scripture, which are verifiably dynamic when applied with solid faith under the lordship of Jesus Christ. The "partnership" is the essential feature of this enabling grace; allowing believers to access Christ's promise of "kingdom keys," and to be assured of the Holy Spirit's readiness to actuate their power in the life of the believer.

Faithful students of the Word of God, and some of today's most respected Christian leaders, have noted some of the primary themes which undergird this spiritual collaboration. A concise presentation of many of these primary themes can be found in the Kingdom Dynamics feature of the *New Spirit-Filled Life Bible*. The *New Spirit-Filled Life Study Guide Series*, is an outgrowth of this Kingdom Dynamics feature that provides a treasury of more in-depth insights on these central truths. This study series offers challenges and insights designed to enable you to understand more readily and to appropriate certain dynamic "Kingdom Keys."

Each study guide has twelve to fourteen lessons, and a number of helpful features have been developed to assist you in your study, each marked by a symbol and heading for easy identification.

✝ Kingdom Key

KINGDOM KEY identifies the foundational Scripture passage for each study session and highlights a basic concept or principle presented in the text along with cross-referenced passages.

Kingdom Life

The KINGDOM LIFE feature is designed to give practical understanding and insight. This feature will assist you in comprehending the truths contained in Scripture and applying them to your day-to-day needs, hurts, relationships, concerns, circumstances, or questions.

Word Wealth

The WORD WEALTH feature provides important definitions of key terms.

Behind the Scenes

BEHIND THE SCENES supplies information about cultural beliefs and practices, doctrinal disputes, and various types of background information that will explicate Bible passages and teachings.

Kingdom Extra

The optional KINGDOM EXTRA feature will guide you to Bible dictionaries, Bible encyclopedias, and other resources that will enable you to gain further insights into a given topic.

Probing the Depths

Finally, PROBING THE DEPTHS will present any controversial issues raised by particular lessons and cite Bible passages and other sources which will assist you in arriving at your own conclusions.

The New Spirit-Filled Life Study Guide is a comprehensive resource presenting study and life application questions and exercises with spaces provided in the study guide to record your answers. These study guides are designed to provide all you need to gain a good, basic understanding of the covered theme and apply biblical counsel to your life. You will need only a heart and mind open to the Holy Spirit's illumination, a prayerful attitude, a pencil and a Bible to complete the studies and apply the truths they contain. However, you may want to have a notebook handy if you plan to expand your study to include the optional KINGDOM EXTRA feature.

The Bible study method used in this series employs four basic steps:

1. *Observation:* What does the text say?
2. *Interpretation:* What is the original meaning of the text?
3. *Correlation:* What light can be shed on this text by other Scripture passages?
4. *Application:* How should my life change in response to the Holy Spirit's teaching in this text?

The New King James Version is the translation used wherever Scripture portions are cited in the *New Spirit-Filled Life Kingdom Dynamics Study Guide* series. Using this translation with this series will make your study easier, but it is certainly not imperative; you will profit through use of any translation you choose.

Through Bible study, you will grow in your essential understanding of the Lord, His kingdom and your place in it; but you need more. Jesus was sent to teach us "all things" (John 14:26; 1 Corinthians 2:13). Rely on the Holy Spirit to guide your study and your application of the Bible's truths. Bathe your study time in prayer as you use this series to learn of Him and His plan for your life. Ask the Spirit of God to illuminate the text, enlighten your mind, humble your will, and your heart. As you explore the Word of God and find the keys to unlock its riches, may the Holy Spirit fill every fiber of your being with the joy and power God longs to share with all His beloved children. Read on diligently. Stay open and submissive to Him. Learn to live your life as the Creator intended. You will not be disappointed. He who promises you is faithful!

ADDITIONAL OBSERVATIONS

INTRODUCTION
Meet the Romans

THE NEW TESTAMENT book of Romans has been heralded as the greatest explanation and defense of the central themes of Christianity found anywhere in the Bible. There are profound theological truths and life-altering power to be found here in Paul's incredible statement of faith.

Keep in mind that Romans was originally a letter penned by Paul to a group of believers whom he had never met. This letter was written specifically to address the needs of Christians in the fledgling Roman church. These believers were living in an idolatrous culture and Christianity was new, alien, and held in contempt by many.

Paul's messages were designed to meet people in their context and lives where they hurt, doubted, celebrated, struggled, worried, shared, complained, married, raised families, suffered, questioned, and died.

To begin this study, set aside at least a week and read the book of Romans without any aids.

Questions:

What characteristics and attitudes seem to have been prevalent in this group of believers?

_____

_____

_____

_____

In what ways can you relate to the Roman church?

_____

_____

_____

_____

What questions have arisen during your initial reading of Paul's letter? You'll want to remember these questions as you work through Romans, so you can find answers to them as you go along.

✎ _____

_____

_____

_____

_____

With this initial overview, what might you expect to glean from the book of Romans that will be of value in your own walk with the Lord?

✎ _____

_____

_____

_____

_____

Behind the Scenes—*All Roads Led to Rome*

In Paul's day Rome dominated the whole Mediterranean. It was the world's most important and most powerful city during the first century.

Rome housed a large Jewish population, one almost the size of the one in Jerusalem. So far, archaeologists have uncovered six Jewish catacombs (underground burial areas). And from the inscriptions in these catacombs, we know there were at least eleven synagogues in Rome.

The Christian population in the city was much smaller, but it was large enough for Roman Emperor Nero to blame and martyr them for a great fire that destroyed much of Rome in A.D. 64. It is believed that Nero himself instigated the fire in order to have a reason to persecute the followers of the Christ. Christian tradition tells us that the apostles Peter and Paul were later two of Nero's other victims.

You may wish to study further about the early Roman Empire in order to more thoroughly understand the context of this book.

SESSION ONE

The Righteousness of God

Romans 1:1–17

2 Corinthians 5:21 "For He made Him who knew no sin to be sin for us, that we might become the righteousness of God in Him."

In the twenty-third chapter of Jeremiah, we read in verse 6 that the Lord will be called "The Lord Our Righteousness." "Yahweh-tsidkenu" is the anglicized Hebrew translation. Understanding this name is essential to our comprehension of the nature of God and all He has done for us.

The word "tsidkenu" has at its root the Hebrew "tsadaq" which means to be justified, to be in right standing, or to be exonerated. Both are legal terms referring to the entire process of justice. Since the Spirit of God assigned this "title" to God, the Father, we know that in all He is and in all He does God is completely just, able to acquit or condemn. He is altogether righteous in and of Himself and the sole source of all righteousness. He is the ultimate judge and His Word is the revealed standard by which He rules.

By our acceptance and appropriation of Jesus' death on our behalf, we are enabled to find positional righteousness. That is, though we may struggle daily with our sin nature, we are made righteous by and through Him. When God looks upon those who have believed in Christ as their Savior, what He sees is the righteousness of Christ Himself imputed by the cross.

Read Jeremiah 23:1–6; 1 Corinthians 1:30, 31; Ephesians 6:13–16.

Questions:

Why do you think God chose this legal term to describe Himself?

✏ _____

_____

_____

How might this "name" change the way in which you relate to God?

✏ _____

_____

_____

Word Wealth—*Righteousness*

Righteousness: Greek *dikaiosune* (dik-ah-yos-oo'-nay); Strong's #1343: meaning to show forth a valid claim in act or character. This word implies innocence, free of offense. It is to be in right standing; to be absolved of guilt. A term taken from the courts, it is God's judicial authority to adjudicate or judge wrongs and offenses. His nature is that of justice. It is His mercy to the guilty when He covers the offense due to the sacrifice He made through Jesus Christ. However, the guilty must confess and repent in order to activate this privilege called grace.

Behind the Scenes

In 1741, Jonathan Edwards, a Calvinist Congregational minister, preached a sermon to a congregation in Connecticut. The result of the sermon was uncontrolled weeping, deep sorrow, and repentance. Although Jonathan Edwards was in no way a gifted orator and actually read the sermon from a written page, this long-remembered "hell fire and brimstone" message marked the beginning of what has become known as the "Great Awakening" in the early colonies of America. The name of the sermon: *Sinners in the Hands of an Angry God*. The effect was a healthy fear of God, a greater understanding of personal faith and the importance of a relationship with Jesus. The result of the Great Awakening was widespread, Holy Spirit-fueled revival which soon spread to distant parts of the world.

Edwards' major message was the holiness of God and the depravity of man, not unlike the beginning of Paul's message to the Roman church.

Probing the Depths

Who among us has not heard disparaging remarks about "hellfire and brimstone" messages? We often hear the assertion that salvation prompted by fear of hell results only in "fire insurance" and has no real life-changing value.

However, the penalty for sin *is* death and those who die in their sin *will* suffer the eternal punishment reserved for satan and his fallen angels. Although the primary message of the gospel is Christ's love and redemption, the fact remains that only the redeemed will escape the deserved punishment of hell. To attempt to ignore or delete this fact serves only to dilute the gospel of Christ and remove the consequence of refusing God's salvation in Christ. We were created to know and serve God, and to be in a loving, intimate relationship with our heavenly Father. Christ came to reinstate that relationship and without it we will die in our sin. The consequence of hell for those who refuse His love is necessary to substantiate the integrity of God as both just *and* loving. The penalty of sin is inherent—it separates us from God.

Jonathan Edwards' sermon, *Sinners in the Hands of an Angry God*, is available in print and on many sites on the Internet. Locate a copy and read it for yourself.

Questions:

Why do you suppose the reaction to this sermon resulted in revival?

_____
_____
_____
_____
_____

Why do you suppose "hellfire and brimstone" preaching has become taboo?

_____
_____
_____
_____
_____

Kingdom Life—*Can God Be Known?*

Paul makes a bold statement in Romans 1:18 and 19. God's righteousness is revealed in His deep-seated anger against humankind, for people wickedly suppress the truth about Him (1:18). God can be known because He reveals Himself in the creation (Psalm 19:1–2) and directly to us. But unrighteousness has hidden Him from the eyes of mankind. We cannot see truth when our eyes are veiled. Only through the Holy Spirit's revelation can we understand righteousness.

The Jewish people assumed that righteousness was theirs, for they possessed the Law of God and thus knew God through revelation. The pagan peoples around them simply stumbled after God in darkness. But Paul makes it clear that no one lives without some knowledge of God. Both Jews and Gentiles had rejected God demonstrating so clearly the need of all for a righteousness that can come only through faith in Jesus Christ.

People are no different today. Rather than turn toward God, people turn away. With their ability to reason darkened by sin, they even stoop to the worship of idols in the form of self, fame, material goods, etc. Society, which we may call the world, rejects God and His people often forget Him in their pursuit of worldly success. The result is the same now as it was in Paul's day: sexual perversion (Romans 1:23–27) and every kind of wickedness expressed through interpersonal relationships (Romans 1:28–31).

Read Romans 1:23–31, 1 John 5:21; 2:15–17.

Questions:

What are the "idols" in your life?

_____

_____

_____

How does this affect your relationship with others?

_____

_____

_____

How does this affect your relationship with the Lord?

_____

_____

_____

_____

_____

God's Plan

The sinful nature of man is endemic. None can escape it and none can change its course. But God instituted a plan for the salvation and redemption of man. His plan was prefigured through the sacrificial rituals and precise laws of the Old Testament. God's answer to the question of the sin problem was evident in symbolisms, one of which is the Tabernacle typology. His solution is enacted and fulfilled through the life, death, resurrection, and ascension of the Christ. The completed redemption of mankind back to right standing and relationship with God is the miracle that makes us the righteousness of God.

And how do we possess this benefit? How can we access it? There's only one way: by faith (Romans 1:17).

The phrase "the righteousness of God" refers to the righteousness that comes from God. Since it comes from Him, it is consistent with His nature and standard. It's a right standing before God that is given to us by God. And it is this right standing that is revealed—unveiled to us "from faith to faith" (1:17). In other words, it starts by faith and continues by faith. Paul highlights this by quoting Habakkuk 2:4: "The just shall live by faith." This Old Testament passage literally reads, "The righteous person in [or by] his faithfulness [firmness, consistency, belief, faith, steadfastness] shall live!" *Shall live* is virtually synonymous with *shall be saved*. A right relationship with God begins with our exercise of trusting faith in Christ and is maintained by our exercise of trusting faith in Christ. God saves and enables us. Nevertheless, we must receive His salvation by faith, and thereby grow and persevere in that salvation through faith.

Read 2 Corinthians 5:1–7; Ephesians 6:16; Ephesians 2:20; Galatians 2:20; Galatians 3:5–7.

Questions:

Describe or define faith in your own words.

_____

_____

_____

What effect should "walking by faith" have on day-to-day life?

_____

_____

_____

How does faith respond to God? To others?

_____

_____

_____

Word Wealth—*Faith*

Faith: Hebrew *pistis* (pis-tis); Strong's #4102: Conviction, confidence, trust, belief, reliance, trustworthiness, and persuasion. In the New Testament setting, pistis is the divinely implanted principle of inward confidence, assurance, trust, and reliance in God and all that He says. The word sometimes denotes the object or content of belief *and* trust.

Kingdom Life—*The Gospel of Salvation*

The word salvation means deliverance, preservation, or rescue. Unfortunately, when most Christians talk about salvation, they mean the *initial* act of placing trust in Jesus as their Savior from sin and as Lord of their life. Paul's understanding of the gospel of salvation is much fuller. Salvation in Christ is total. It covers every aspect of our lives from the moment we trust in Christ throughout the rest of our earthly sojourn and including our entire life of bliss in eternity. It involves salvation from the penalty of sin (which is death here and forever), from the power of sin (which shackles us to death here and forever), and from the presence of sin (which seeks to slap us in the face with death here and forever). The Lord justifies us, freeing us from sin's penalty (Romans 3:21—5:21); sanctifies us, freeing us from sin's power (6:1—8:16), and glorifies us, freeing us from sin's presence (8:17–30). And He saves all of us— not just our souls or spirits but also our bodies (8:23; 1 Thessalonians 5:23). He leaves nothing unredeemed. Every bit of us is washed, cleansed, made righteous, healed, transformed. So salvation is at once, an event, a process, and a completed work. Salvation is a process of deliverance and healing that begins when we choose to believe in, accept and surrender to the lordship of Jesus Christ. It is generated through the renewing of our mind through the truth of the Scriptures, and the transformation of our hearts. We are continuously *being* saved until we meet Jesus face-to-face. What the Bible presents is a *whole* gospel for the *whole* world that covers *whole*ness for each person throughout his or her *whole* life.

Read 2 Corinthians 2:15; 2 Corinthians 3:17; 1 John 3:2.

Questions:

In what ways do you experience salvation as a process?

_____

_____

_____

_____

What do the words "from glory to glory" mean to you?

_____

_____

_____

_____

How might this change your outlook on life?

_____

_____

_____

_____

Record Your Thoughts

In light of what you have learned in this session, reread the first 16 verses of Romans chapter one.

Questions:

What do you now understand by Paul's statement: "the righteousness of God is revealed from faith to faith"?

✎_____

_____

_____

How does this change your concept of salvation?

✎_____

_____

_____

How will righteousness change the way you relate to God and the world around you?

✎_____

_____

_____

Session Two

Guilty As Charged

Romans 1:18—2:16

✝ **Kingdom Key—*All Have Sinned***

Romans 3:22, 23 . . . For there is no difference, for all have sinned and fall short of the glory of God . . .

We have already seen that God's righteousness—a right standing before Him that only He can give—comes through the gospel, the good news about salvation by faith through God's Son, Jesus Christ (Romans 1:16, 17). But this presupposes that we need God's righteousness. As a result of the fall of man into sin, our relationship with our Creator has been so severely damaged that we cannot repair it. Nothing we could do would ever put things right between us and our Holy God. So God had to step in and initiate what we couldn't.

What happened? What did the human race do that was so offensive to the One who made us? How did we fall out of a right standing with the Lord? Like a prosecuting attorney pressing the case for God, Paul sets out the evidence of our wrongdoing for us to see. The portrait is grim and convincing. It clearly shows that the case against us is ironclad; we are definitely guilty.

Read Romans 2:11–16.

Questions:

Consider Paul's words, "there is no partiality with God" (v. 11). What insight does this give of God's nature?

✎ _____

_____

_____

In what way should this impact your life?

_____

_____

_____

_____

_____

Word Wealth—*Sin*

Sin: Hebrew *hamartia* (ham-ar-tee-ah); Strong's #266: Literally, "missing the mark," failure, offense, taking the wrong course, wrongdoing, sin, guilt. The New Testament uses the word in a generic sense for concrete wrongdoing (John 8:34; John 8:46; 2 Corinthians 11:7); as a principle and quality of action (Romans 5:12,13,20; Hebrews 3:13); and as a sinful deed (Matthew 12:31; Acts 7:60; 1 John 5:16).

The Heavens Are Declaring

Paul tolerates no excuses as to recognition of God's existence and preeminence. He confronts any attempt to defend ourselves as uninformed in verses 18–21. God has revealed Himself in all that He has created—we have no excuse.

But, not only do we attempt to make excuses on the human level, we also try to make them in the spiritual realm. We claim ignorance and expect to be exonerated of all guilt. But God has revealed Himself clearly to all and continues to do so daily in all that He has created and in all that He has decreed. But unredeemed eyes are blinded by sin, by satan.

Paul describes the thinking of those who recognize God as "futile" and "foolish." He also says that God will give them "up to uncleaness" and "vile passions" and "over to a debased mind." Sounds very much like the world we live in, does it not? How very sad that it can also describe those who dwell in the body of Christ. Even though we see and know Him as God, we often choose to act and think otherwise.

Read Psalm 19:1–9.

Questions:

What does the physical creation itself reveal or tell us about the Creator? What is it silent about?

✎ _____

_____

_____

Has any of this evidence been used by the Holy Spirit to help convince you or someone you know of who God is and that He really lives? If so, recount what happened.

✎ _____

_____

_____

In what ways have you failed to recognize God in your own life?

✎ _____

_____

_____

How has this adversely affected your life and relationships?

✎ _____

_____

_____

Kingdom Life—*Tough Love*

Paul says that God is really angry about human "ungodliness and unrighteousness" (1:18). Ungodliness depicts a character that does not reflect God's character (thinking, being, and behaving), and unrighteousness describes the breach it causes in our relationship with both man and God.

God's wrath is invoked by man's purposeful denial and rejection of His pre-eminence and right to rule the world He created. God's wrath, however, has at its source His immense love for man. It is His love that causes His intense desire for man to be reconciled to Him. The only true life that is available to man is obtained in right relationship to God. That life is God's will for us and His anger is ignited when we refuse life and choose death—the death of living outside the experience of God's presence in our lives.

God's anger is also aroused when we live disconnected from self and others. It may be sin, brokenness, or self-centered views that cause us to choose separation, thereby minimizing the intended beauty, joy, and richness of sharing God in fellowship with others.

Read Romans 1:18–23; Psalm 19:1–6; Acts 14:17; 17:22–30; Romans 2:14, 15.

Questions:

Why do you think our human relationships matter so much to God?

_____

_____

_____

What do these verses say to those who claim "all paths lead to the same God"?

_____

_____

_____

Worshipping any but the One True God is idolatry. In what ways is idolatry alive and well today?

_____

_____

_____

Are there any false gods in your own life?

_____

_____

_____

Wrath of God: God's righteous and just anger against anything that twists or distorts His intended purpose and thereby violates and offends His holy, moral character.

Ungodliness: A lack of proper reverence toward God, in terms of rebellion as well as neglect.

Unrighteousness: The injustices perpetrated between human beings in their dealings with each other.

Suppress the truth: "Hold down"—rationalize away or try to excuse or conceal—the true facts about oneself, others, God, or anything else.

When God Gives Up

Throughout the latter part of Romans 1, Paul wraps his indictment of the human race around a single idea: God giving people up to increased immorality (vv. 24, 26, 28). You see, when people substitute false or demonic gods for the real God—the One we know truly exists and deserves our gratitude and praise—they make their "gods" the standard for what's right and wrong, or true and false. In effect, they have put themselves in the place of God. When this is done by any of us, God permits us to exercise our new station in life; He gives us up to our own foolishness and lets us set our own standards for thought and behavior. The result is a tragic, destructive mess.

Read Romans 1:24–32.

Create a chart for yourself with two columns. In the left-hand column, record what happens when God gives people up to their idolatrous desires.

Godless Attributes	Godly Attributes

Now take each negative and write down its positive in the right-hand column. For example, the opposite of uncleanness (v. 24) is cleanness, and the positive opposite of (evil) lusts of the heart (v. 24) is good desires of the heart. These positives will help you see what God wants His people to be like in contrast to those who set themselves up against Him by serving false gods.

Kingdom Life—*Judge Not*

In the opening lines of chapter two, Paul turns the case against rebellious humankind to our most common characteristic—hypocrisy.

- Hypocrisy is a repulsive trait that is universally considered to be unacceptable.
- Hypocrisy is nothing more than a lie. To be hypocritical is to be "hyper-critical."
- Hypocrisy is the self-righteous judgment of another. It is the pretence of righteousness passing judgment based upon self-serving ends.
- Hypocrisy is the blind claiming sight; the ungodly asserting the right to judge.

Read Romans 2:1–10; Matthew 7:1–5.

Questions:

What is God's reaction to hypocrisy?

_____

_____

_____

_____

What are examples of hypocrisy in your own life?

_____

_____

_____

_____

How has this affected your spiritual life?

How has this affected your human relationships?

How can you guard against this in the future?

Behind the Scenes

At first glance, Romans 2:7 and 10 seem to teach that salvation is by works. But that cannot be true since it would contradict what Paul himself says elsewhere in Romans (3:21–28; 4:1–8). So what do these two verses teach? Their central point is that God judges impartially. For those who show themselves to be self-centered and doers of evil—in other words, unsaved people—He will judge them appropriately and rightly, pouring out His wrath upon them. Whether they are Jews or Gentiles, it makes no difference. Likewise, those who demonstrate their true nature as children of God by doing good and seeking His kingdom will receive the fruit of their relationship to Him and labor for Him—eternal life. And this they will have regardless of their racial or national status, "For there is no partiality with God" (v. 11). Put another way, we are saved by faith; but living, true faith always produces good works. Otherwise, it is a lifeless, false faith.

Read Ephesians 2:8, 9; Titus 3:5; James 2:14–26.

Questions:

What does a living, true faith look like?

_____

_____

_____

_____

_____

It has been said that faith is an active verb; what does this mean to you?

_____

_____

_____

_____

_____

In what ways is this active faith evidenced in your own life?

_____

_____

_____

_____

_____

All Will Be Judged

God will judge everyone: their actions, motives, thoughts, words . . . you name it, everything will come under the Judge's all-knowing scrutiny. And none of us, not one single person, will be able to survive His judgment. That's bad, but not all bad. Because those of us who repent and by faith accept His gracious provision of total, eternal forgiveness through Jesus Christ will find the Judge on our side. Rather than His gavel coming down with a sentence of everlasting death, He'll embrace us as a loving Father would His children and give us an incorruptible inheritance of everlasting life with Him.

We have already considered the importance of being reminded of the consequence of unforgiven sin. It is in the fact of God's righteous judgment that the value of that reminder is revealed. We will all be judged, but God will not remember the trespasses of those whose sin is covered by the blood of Jesus, the Lamb of God. That's good news, even great news! So Paul relates to us *bad* news in order to motivate us toward hearing and receiving the *good* news!

Record Your Thoughts

It is so very easy to point a finger at the unbelieving world and claim that this portion of God's word indicts them. But we have just learned that the very finger that points toward others accuses the one to whom the finger belongs.

Questions:

What truths have truly impacted you in this session?

✎ _____

_____

_____

_____

_____

What changes have these realizations prompted?

✎ _____

_____

_____

_____

_____

How will your relationships—with God and others—change as a result?

✎ _____

_____

_____

_____

_____

SESSION THREE

God Has Made a Way
Romans 2:17—3:20

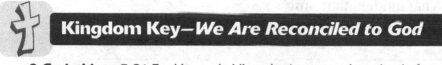

Kingdom Key—*We Are Reconciled to God*

2 Corinthians 5:21 For He made Him who knew no sin to *be* sin for us, that we might become the righteousness of God in Him.

We have been reconciled to God by the ultimate sacrifice of our Lord, Jesus Christ. Though He was impeccably innocent and sin was far from Him, He voluntarily took upon Himself *all* the sin of *all* mankind for *all* time. He died our death; the death that we earned as the consequence of sin.

Reconciliation is the process by which God and man are brought together again. This is made possible through the blood of Jesus, which demonstrates the power and the model for reconciliation. We were once estranged from God, but we have been brought to Him and restored to relationship through the shed blood of Christ; His power is fueled in us through the body of His flesh through His death. As children of God and joint heirs with Jesus Christ, we are enjoined to follow the standard He left for us—to be reconciled to God and with each other as He reconciled us to God. As we model His ministry of reconciliation, the world will be impacted.

Read also Isaiah 53; John 17:20, 21.

Questions:
Why does Scripture call Jesus "a Man of sorrows"?

_____

_____

_____

Do you see the unity Christ prayed for alive in the church today?

_____

_____

_____

_____

What hinders that unity?

_____

_____

_____

_____

In what ways do you enter into this unity?

_____

_____

_____

_____

In what ways do you attempt to live out the desired unity of and with Christ?

_____

_____

_____

_____

Word Wealth—*Reconciled*

Reconciled: Greek *katallasso* (kat-ul-las'-so); Strong's #2644: To change, exchange, re-establish, restore relationships, make things right, remove an enmity. Five times the Word of God refers to God reconciling us to Himself through the life, death, and resurrection of His Son Jesus. Whether speaking of God and man or husband and wife, *katallosso* describes the reestablishing of a proper, loving, interpersonal relationship, which has been broken or disrupted.

Kingdom Life—*We Have No Excuse*

We are not only without excuse before God, but we are all guilty before Him. We have violated His standard of righteousness. Not a single one of us has ever done otherwise. Therefore, just as Paul tells the Jews in Rome, law-keeping will not save us; it will not justify us before Him. Instead, the Law exposes us, showing us that we are *all* sinners, *all* lawbreakers, *all* of us are criminals. No exceptions!

So for now, we need to understand the charge against us, consider the evidence, and weigh the consequences. And when we do, our counterarguments fall to the ground. We are left silent, dumbstruck. Without the Judge's mercy, without the Father's reaching out to His prodigals in love and grace, every one of us is utterly without hope, trapped and condemned in our own sin.

Read Psalm 14:1–4; 53:1–5.

Questions:

Consider the words Paul quotes from the book of Psalms, "there is no fear of God before their eyes." What are your thoughts?

_____

_____

_____

_____

How do you reconcile the gracious mercy of God and the "fear of God"?

_____

_____

_____

How might the fear of God change your outlook on life?

_____

_____

_____

_____

_____

How might the fear of God change the way in which you relate to others?

_____

_____

_____

_____

_____

Children of the Kingdom

Read Luke 15:11–32.

The scribes and Pharisees were self-deceived. Like the prodigal son's elder brother, they saw no need of repentance, for they believed they were already "righteous." They thought they were already "sons of the kingdom." But their cynical and jealous posture to Jesus' response to "sinners" invalidated their claim. If they were truly "sons of God's kingdom" they would, like their heavenly Father, rejoice over lost "sinners" returning to His family. Contrast the father's attitude toward the returning son with the boy's older brother's.

Clearly the kingdom of God is not to be confused with any other kingdom, including the kingdom of Israel. "Insiders" thrown out and "outsiders" invited into the kingdom! Religious heritage and ritual are not to be confused with spiritual regeneration and rebirth. True children of the kingdom are those whose belief in and acceptance of Jesus' sacrifice on their behalf has granted them release from the power of sin and death and transference into the kingdom of light and life. They are those whom the Father has qualified to receive His inheritance.

Questions:

How do you experience the "power of darkness" in your own life?

_____

_____

_____

_____

What is the inheritance of the children of the kingdom of God?

_____

_____

_____

_____

Do others recognize you as a child of God?

_____

_____

_____

_____

What changes need to happen in your own life for others to recognize you as a "saint in the light"?

_____

_____

_____

_____

Probing the Depths

Perhaps one of the most unique and amazing characteristics of God is that He is a forgiving God. We saw how the parable of the prodigal son reveals the forgiving heart of God our Father. Such a spirit of forgiveness is, therefore, to characterize His children.

Read Micah 7:18, 19; 6:14, 15; Matthew 18:15–35.

No experience transcends that of forgiveness. God completely "let it go" when in His great mercy He cancelled the entire debt our sins had incurred. Amazing grace! Why, then, do we find it so difficult to "let it go" when a brother or sister offends us? Could it be we have not really understood the size and significance of the debt God in Christ forgave us? Sometimes we are halfhearted in forgiving those who have sinned against us. We say, "I'll forgive, but I won't forget!" But that is forgiving from the head, not from the heart! What if God forgave us like that? True forgiveness: "lets it go" completely . . . no digging up of the past. "But you don't know how deeply I've been hurt!" we cry. Hurt more deeply than Jesus was by our sins? If He can forgive, so can we. Further, in giving forgiveness we are simply giving what we have already received—His forgiveness!

It's important to stress that, for us, forgiveness is a process and may not always be accomplished in the blink of an eye. After we have forgiven all offenses and hurts we are conscious of, God may reveal a deeper level of pain, as we are emotionally able to handle it, in order to lead us to complete freedom—one step at a time. The point is that we must 1) choose to begin the forgiveness process and 2) respond immediately to those new areas of pain that the Lord may surface through time. Then, as we continue to "give it up" to Jesus, its power over our memories will gradually be released until we are no longer tormented by those painful memories of our past experience.

Questions:

Is there any unforgiveness in your own heart?

_____

_____

_____

_____

_____

What impact has this had in your life and in other relationships?

✎_____

_____

_____

_____

_____

Word Wealth—*Forgiving*

Forgiving: Greek *charizomai* (kahr-id-zahm-ahee); Strong's #5483: To do a favor, show kindness unconditionally, give freely, grant forgiveness, forgive freely, unconditional favor freely and mercifully shown. The word is from the same root as the word for "grace" (*charis*).

Forgiveness from the heart does not keep a score of wrongs. It "remembers to forget"! True forgiveness is a spirit, not a statistic. Heart forgiveness is like God's forgiveness—it is always available when needed. Surely such a spirit of forgiveness must come from the Spirit of God. Clearly, "to err [sin] is human, but to forgive is divine." Thus, forgiveness, unlimited and heartfelt, can only come from God Himself . . . and it has in Christ! And so we are commanded to treat others as we have been treated. We are to "be kind to one another, tenderhearted, forgiving one another, even as God in Christ forgave you" (Ephesians 4:32).

Transformation

Read 2 Corinthians 3:17; 5:15, 17; 1 John 4:12; 5:18–20.

The kingdom of God consists of transformed people. They think differently, they see differently, they hear differently, they act differently. In a word, they live differently—because they *are* different!

When we have truly repented of self-focused living and have fully believed the good news of Jesus Christ, we will no longer live for ourselves, but we will live for the King of the kingdom, our Lord. We are "in Him," and He is in us. Therefore we are "a new creation:" a totally new being that did not exist before.

Jesus has called us as His followers to self-denying discipleship, to a process of profound transformation. As citizens of God's kingdom, disciples of Jesus Christ increasingly are to reflect the character of the One under whose authority they have come and within whose kingdom they live. The character of the King and His kingdom becomes their character.

Questions:

In what ways to do you recognize this "transformation" in your own life?

_____

_____

_____

_____

What effect would a truly transformed life have on values and priorities?

_____

_____

_____

_____

How might relationships change for those who live as a new creation?

_____

_____

_____

_____

_____

Record Your Thoughts

We have been purchased by the shed blood of Christ. We are now righteous in the eyes of God and are daily being transformed into the image of our Lord.

Questions:

How do you see this process being lived out in your own life?

_____

_____

_____

_____

How might unforgiveness hinder this process?

_____

_____

_____

_____

Do you experience God's promise of being "partakers" of His kingdom in your daily life?

_____

_____

_____

_____

Why do you believe this is so?

_____

_____

_____

_____

ADDITIONAL OBSERVATIONS

We Are Made Worthy
Romans 3:21—4:25

Kingdom Key—*We Are Justified by Faith*

Galatians 3:16 ". . . knowing that a man is not justified by the works of the law but by faith in Jesus Christ . . ."

"There is none righteous, no, not one," declares Romans 3:10, establishing that all people are unrighteous and therefore deserving of judgment. But God's covenant love reaches beyond the fulfillment of justice to establish a bond of fellowship in the blood of Jesus Christ. Faith in His blood brings our deliverance from the wrath of God. Because of Christ's atoning work we now stand before the Father as righteous! Justification also opens the door to victorious living through participation in Jesus' life as we are in Him and together comprise the body of Christ. This is the essence of "justification."

What does it mean to be justified? It is a conferred state of innocence—"just as if I'd" never sinned.

Read Acts 13:38, 39; 1 Corinthians 6:9–11; Galatians 2:16–20; James 2:20–26.

Questions:

Once we are justified by the atoning work of Christ, how are we seen by God?

_____

_____

_____

_____

_____

How do you reconcile our continuing sin nature and justification?

✏️_____

_____

_____

_____

Our lives should demonstrate the change that God has worked in us through justification, yet we all fall short. What action should you take to remedy this in your own life?

✏️_____

_____

_____

_____

_____

Word Wealth—*Justified*

Justified: Hebrew *dikaioo* (dik-ah-yah'-oh); Strong's #1344: A legal term signifying to acquit, declare righteous, show to be righteous. It is to be rendered or regarded as innocent, to be proclaimed free of guilt.

Kingdom Life—*He's Never Far Away*

Just as the prodigal son ran from love and security, we too, are runaways. Determined to chase our dreams our way, we ran from infinite Love. And like the prodigal, we have found that our way is not the better way. Our lives have not improved. Although we may occasionally experience gain; it is never permanent, and something about it always rings hollow. We know we were meant for something better, much better.

But we'll never find that something on the run. Someday, somehow, we'll have to come to the end of ourselves and turn back to God. It may seem we have a long, hard journey back to our Father; but God has never ceased longing for our return. He has never ceased to call our name and to desire that our relationship with Him be set right. When we finally turn back to Him, we will not be met with anger or condemnation; on the contrary, the blessings of heaven will pour over us and wrap around us, restoring our hearts, transforming our minds, healing our souls of hurts and injustices.

Questions:

What is the difference between "godly sorrow" and the "sorrow of the world"?

_____

_____

_____

_____

_____

In what ways has "godly sorrow" led to healing in your own life?

_____

_____

_____

_____

_____

Have you ever shared this with others? If so, to what effect?

_____

_____

_____

_____

Word Wealth—*Repent*

Repent: Greek *metanoeo* (met-an-ah-eh'-oh); Strong's #3340: From *meta,* meaning "after," and *noeo,* meaning "to think." Repentance is a decision that results in a change of mind, which in turn leads to a change of purpose and action.

Turn Toward Life

The first call of the kingdom is to repentance. The implications of biblical repentance are threefold: 1) renunciation and reversal, 2) submission and humility (willingness to learn), and 3) continual malleability. There is no birth into the kingdom without hearing the call to salvation, renouncing one's sin and turning from sin toward Christ the Savior.

Read Acts 3:19.

Questions:

What are the "times of refreshing" to which Paul refers?

_____

_____

_____

_____

_____

Have you ever experienced the "presence of the Lord"?

_____

_____

_____

_____

_____

What may hinder this experience in your life?

_____

_____

_____

_____

_____

Words of Life

Paul uses four crucial words in this section of Romans whose definitions contain much of the power of the gospel of Christ.

Justification: We have already seen that justification results in the conferred state that makes it "just as if I'd" never sinned. Justification is a divine act whereby sinners are *declared,* not made, righteous.

Grace: This Greek word (*charis*) shares the same root as the Greek word for joy (*chara*) and rejoice (*chairo*). *Charis* causes rejoicing. *Charis* is God's free gift of unmerited favor and undeserved blessing.

Redemption: To be redeemed is to be set free—at a price. It is a release secured by the payment of a ransom. Christ paid the price for our freedom. Without His death on our behalf, we would still be held captive by sin and death.

Propitiation: To propitiate is to gain or regain favor or goodwill. Propitiation is a satisfactory answer affected by a sacrificial offering, removing God's wrath and judgment. Christ death made propitiation for our sins.

 Kingdom Extra

The theme of Christ's shedding of blood for our benefit is a central one in the New Testament. Its roots go all the way back to Genesis 3:21, where God spilled the first innocent animal blood to provide clothing for Adam and Eve after they sinned against Him.

See how many Old Testament events you can recall that recount the shedding of innocent blood to deal with someone's wrongdoing. If you're unfamiliar with the Old Testament, you may want to consult a Bible dictionary or Bible encyclopedia and look up the articles on blood, atonement, sacrifices, and the death of Christ.

When loaded with this background information, turn to Isaiah 53, Hebrews 9 and 10, and 1 Peter 1:17–19 to see more fully how precious Jesus' shed blood is and what it has accomplished for us.

 **Kingdom Life—*Arrogance***

Arrogance is an insidious thing. It infects everything it touches. It seeps into the bloodstream of gratitude, compliment, accomplishment, or social or religious standing, then slowly contaminates humility while injecting stronger doses of snobbery until its victims really begin to believe that they are better than others and therefore feel entitled to anything, even in the name of religion at times.

This disease turns especially deadly when it grows in Christians. It sets believers against believers, destroying the church's unity. It turns unbelievers away from God in disgust of the tainted witness of the Church.

Those suffering the effects of an arrogant, prideful heart have a hard time recognizing and owning it. The tendency is to be least self-aware, or failure to know their spiritual vulnerabilities. Some of the tell-tale signs of arrogance are: a condescending attitude, prejudice of any form, difficulty expressing genuine thankfulness, difficulty admitting a need for help, a tendency to boast in accomplishments, position or power, feeling entitled to attention, and a begrudging attitude toward God, and what He does or does not do for you.

None of us escapes this disease, and the earlier it's detected and combated the better. So, don't treat this issue lightly. Arrogance is at the heart of hypocrisy; and the gospel of justification by faith cuts out hypocrisy's lifeblood.

Read James 4:6; Matthew 23:12–36.

Questions:

Arrogance and pride are bosom companions. What do you think it means that God resists the proud?

_____

_____

_____

_____

In Jesus' admonition to the Pharisees, he mentions many offenses. In what ways do you see these attitudes in action today?

_____

_____

_____

_____

In light of the list of tell-tale signs above, do you find any of these characteristics in your own life?

✎ _____

_____

_____

_____

Probing the Depths

In building his case for justification by faith, Paul assumes his readers know who Abraham was and what he did. Read his story in Genesis 11:27—25:11. Even if you are familiar with the events of Abraham's life, take some time to get reacquainted with it.

If you explore these verses, pay particular attention to the passages that tell of the promise God made to Abraham, how Abraham responded, how and when the promise took effect, and when Abraham was finally circumcised. You will find that Paul's use of Abraham makes his case for justification by faith apart from circumcision absolutely airtight.

Questions:

What is the significance of Abraham's story for future generations, including us?

✎ _____

_____

_____

_____

How should this impact your day-to-day life?

✎ _____

_____

_____

_____

Kingdom Extra

Have you ignored the Old Testament? Do you think it's irrelevant or that the New Testament supersedes it? Don't miss out on anything God wants to give you. Commit today to balance your study time between the Old and New Testaments. Perhaps that will involve reading one chapter a day out of each Testament, or maybe during your study time through Romans you can commit to spending a little extra time looking up the references given to the Old Testament and pondering them a bit longer than you otherwise would. Whatever approach you take, make it realistic, then stick with it, bathing your time in prayer so the Holy Spirit can teach you, guide you, and strengthen your soul in the everlasting, absolute truth.

Record Your Thoughts

Questions:

Considering all you have now read about justification, what message have you received regarding guilt for past wrongs?

_____

_____

_____

_____

How should the reality of God's justification through Jesus' sacrifice affect your self-image?

_____

_____

_____

_____

In what ways do you fail to experience the freedom of this gift in your life?

_____

_____

_____

_____

What can you do to change that?

_____

_____

_____

_____

_____

ADDITIONAL OBSERVATIONS

Life from Death

Romans 5:1–21

Kingdom Key—We Are Delivered

Colossians 1:13, 14 "He has delivered us from the power of darkness and conveyed us into the kingdom of the Son of His love, in whom we have redemption through His blood, the forgiveness of sins."

The word translated here as "conveyed" is the Greek *methistemi* (meth-is'-tay-mee). It means to transfer, exchange, or translate. The root of this word denotes: a continual abiding, a staunchly established appointment, a covenantal standing. The word suggests an immutable, everlasting transfer.

We have been delivered from the "power of darkness" and all the effects of that darkness: hopelessness, despair, fear, and death. We have been translated, changed, eternally transferred into the kingdom of God through Jesus Christ. We now live in a kingdom filled with faith, hope, love, and life. We now have access to all the riches of God's kingdom. To access the wealth of the kingdom, we only need to choose to accept, moment by moment, the life made available to us by the sacrifice of Jesus—He died that we might live, abundantly!

Read John 10:10; Galatians 2:18.

Questions:

How would you define "abundant life"?

Does this describe your walk with the Lord?

✎ _____

_____

_____

_____

Do you know experientially that you have been conveyed, translated, transformed?

✎ _____

_____

_____

_____

If all aspects of our walk with the Lord are progressive (as we have learned earlier), how does that fact impact our translation into the kingdom?

✎ _____

_____

_____

_____

Paradoxical Perspective

As we begin this section, it is important that we understand paradox. Paradoxes, as used in Scripture, are pregnant with meaning, but they can truly challenge our minds. They present us with truths that appear to have no way of being true and are totally alien to our experience. Paradoxes seem to contradict themselves. One wonders why God would choose to communicate in such a seemingly complicated way.

We know that God exists in the spiritual realm, a dimension beyond the physical world. To attempt to impose the limits, restrictions and expectations of our world on the spiritual realm is senseless. It is a place and a state of being that is simply "other." It is a place of the eternal, a concept beyond our limited intellect.

When God communicates eternal truth to us, our language and earthbound minds limit our ability to receive the message. By speaking in ways that seem contradictory to our experience, God challenges us to reach beyond our limited understanding and enter into that spiritual realm.

As we ponder and explore the paradoxes of Scripture, we inevitably discover they are true, that they provide insight into reality we have never seen before. Consequently, they tend to transform our perspective, and in so doing, they usually change our motivations and the way we behave.

Read Luke 22:24–30; Ephesians 5:21–33; 6:5–9; Matthew 6:19–21; Luke 12:13–34; 1 Timothy 6:17–19.

Questions:

What are some ways the paradoxes in Scripture have proven true in your own life?

_____

_____

_____

Kingdom Life—*Justification Is Accomplished*

Paul writes, "having been justified by faith, we have . . ." (5:1). Did you notice that Paul's words tell us that the act of being justified is a *past* fact? Once we place our trust in Jesus Christ, God declares we are now rightly related to Him. The legal matter of justification is done, over with, fully accomplished. We have been declared righteous, forgiven of our sins. All that remains is for this righteousness to become an active force in our daily lives.

Paul wants to tell us what justification brings to us. It not only sets us right with God; there are many other blessings that flow from it, such as: peace, access to grace (God's unmerited favor), glory in tribulations (pressures, distresses, hardships, sufferings), character (quality produced through enduring tribulations), hope, love, salvation, joy, reconciliation, righteousness, eternal life.

Read James 2:18–24.

Questions:

Justification is an accomplished fact in the life of a believer. Why then, does James speak of the power of "works"?

✎_____

_____

_____

Does your life show forth the blessings of justification?

✎_____

_____

_____

_____

Where do you fall short?

✎_____

_____

_____

_____

How does this hinder your relationships with God and man?

✎_____

_____

_____

_____

Probing the Depths

What an interesting concept it is to "glory in tribulations." Suffering is painful and would seemingly result in something opposite of glory. It seems we have come upon one of those kingdom paradoxes. Tribulation can bring all manner of fear, anxiety, and sorrow; but God will so fill our hearts that even the worst of circumstances pale in the light of His glory in our lives.

Read 2 Thessalonians 1:3–5; James 1:2–4.

Questions:

What is your common response to suffering?

✎_____

_____

_____

_____

Can you think of a time when you were going through hardship and you were able to praise God in the midst of it?

✎_____

_____

_____

_____

What led to your praises?

✎_____

_____

_____

_____

Kingdom Life—*Love Never Fails*

It's easy to love someone who loves you back. But what about loving someone who turns on you, who openly defies your standards, slanders you, betrays your loyalty, takes advantage of your generosity, lies to you, steals the credit you deserve, even turns others against you? Only by the power of God at work in our lives can we offer love to such a one. But even then, would you be able to sacrifice your life for that person?

But God sent His Son to do just that—to die for those who denied, defied and reviled Him. Jesus, on behalf of the triune Godhead: Father, Son, and Holy Spirit, loving us infinitely and in unity, willingly carried out a monumental plan to save us rebels from our path of self-destruction. No one can force deity to do anything deity doesn't want to do. We didn't deserve this unconditional, sacrificial expression of love. We spurned it with everything God had given us! Nevertheless, Love responded to our need, spread His innocent arms wide on a rugged cross, and embraced our punishment so we could enjoy everlasting forgiveness and unending bliss as restored, redeemed citizens of His unimaginable kingdom.

Don't wait a moment longer. Turn your eyes toward heaven; and in response to this great act of infinite Love, "rejoice in God through our Lord Jesus Christ . . . by the Holy Spirit who was given to us" (vv. 11, 5).

Meet the Adam Family

Now we come to the heart of Romans 5, perhaps even the crux of the entire letter of Romans. In ten verses (vv. 12–21), Paul summarizes the history of redemption, from the event that made it necessary to the event that stands at its apex. He does it by comparing the first Adam, who precipitated the Fall of the entire human race, with the Second Adam, who has made it possible for all human beings to enjoy everlasting life with God, if they will respond to the Lord by faith. The first Adam brought death through his life; the Second Adam brought life through His death. That's the profound paradox and point of Romans 5.

With this background information in mind, read through Romans 5:12–21 and fill in the chart below. The left column deals with the first Adam, the one who disobeyed his Creator in Genesis 3. The right column concerns the Second Adam, the One who has never disobeyed His heavenly Father. Note the similarities and differences. You may discover some real surprises.

The First Adam	The Second Adam
Similarities	
✎_____	_____
_____	_____
_____	_____
_____	_____
_____	_____

The First Adam	The Second Adam

Differences

✎_____   _____

_____   _____

_____   _____

_____   _____

Behind the Scenes

Sin is a disease. It infects every human being from the moment of conception, and it always leads to death—alienation from God, from self, from others, from creation, from physical life, and, if one is careless, from spiritual life as well. There's only one cure. Everything else is only a bandage. And the cure is found in Romans 5:12–21.

Read Genesis, chapters 1—3.

Questions:

Describe the disease of sin.

✎_____

_____

_____

What words most characterize the actions of Adam and Eve?

✎_____

_____

In this list, do you find any attitudes that ever find expression in your own life?

✎_____

_____

Kingdom Extra

Paul refers to Adam as a "type" of Christ. The term *type* refers to a "form, figure, pattern, example." When types are found in Scripture, they are historical persons, events, things, or institutions that prefigure or foreshadow persons, events, things, or institutions yet to come in God's plan. Types are prophetic as well as predictive. They depict not only someone or something that has already played a role in history but someone or something that *will yet* play a role in history. In Romans 5, Paul uses Adam as a prefigure of Jesus Christ. In certain ways, Adam and his actions foretell certain truths about Jesus Christ. But these truths, as Paul lays them out, are negative on Adam's side but positive on Jesus' side. In other words, Adam is a type of Christ because he failed to do in a perfect environment what Jesus did successfully in a sin-ridden environment. So Paul contrasts Adam and Jesus far more than he compares them.

Over the centuries of biblical studies, many other types have been found in the Bible. Below are pairs of Scriptures that give some of the types that have been identified. You may want to look these up and reap for yourself the insight they contain.

Old Testament Type	New Testament Fulfillment
Genesis 7; 8	1 Peter 3:20, 21
Genesis 15:1–6	Romans 4:16–25

Old Testament Type	**New Testament Fulfillment**
Exodus 20:8–11	Hebrews 4:3–10

_____

_____

_____

_____

_____

Leviticus 17:11	1 Peter 1:18, 19

_____

_____

_____

_____

Numbers 12:7	Hebrews 3:1–6

_____

_____

_____

_____

Numbers 21:4–9	John 3:14, 15

_____

_____

_____

_____

John 1; 2	Matthew 12:39, 40

_____

_____

_____

_____

Kingdom Life—*Faith Unto Life*

Romans 5:17 encapsulates for us the effect of both Adam and Jesus on the whole of the human race. A greater contrast has never been known.

"For if by the one man's offense death reigned through the one, much more those who receive abundance of grace and of the gift of righteousness will reign in life through the one, Jesus Christ."

Adam is characterized by disobedience, while Christ is characterized by obedience. We are in Adam by birth, but we are in Christ by faith. In Adam we are condemned to die, but because of Christ's redemptive work, we can be justified and live if we are in Him by faith.

Record Your Thoughts

Questions:

What paradoxical truths have you encountered thus far in your study of Romans?

✎_____

_____

_____

What truths have you discovered that you wish to apply to your life?

✎_____

_____

_____

How has your attitude about death changed?

✎_____

_____

_____

Spend some time considering the imminent return of Christ and your reaction to that reality.

✎_____

_____

_____

How does the truth you have learned thus far in this study impact your closest relationships?

✎_____

_____

_____

How have these truths affected your response to those you don't like? Those you don't know?

✎_____

_____

_____

ADDITIONAL OBSERVATIONS

Bound by Freedom

Romans 6:1—7:25

 Kingdom Key—*We Choose Our Master*

Joshua 24:15 ". . . choose for yourselves this day whom you will serve, . . . But as for me and my house, we will serve the Lord."

A person is a servant or a slave of that to which he gives obedience or that which he recognizes as his master. If he obeys the commands of sin, then sin is his master and he is moving in the direction of eternal death, all the while experiencing a deathlike existence in his present life here and now. If he obeys the commands of righteousness, then he serves righteousness as his master, and he experiences true life, now and in the world to come.

Read Galatians 7:22, 23; John 15:20.

Questions:

What qualities found in a slave are we to possess as children of the kingdom?

✎ _____

_____

_____

What qualities exist within you that are decidedly not slave-like?

✎ _____

_____

_____

The Call of Freedom

Freedom; people move away from their homelands looking for it, others blaze new trails, facing unknown dangers in the pursuit of it. Many fight against addictions just for a taste of it. Far too many die on native or foreign soil in defense of it. More and more people seek to find it in financial independence. Untold numbers have turned to every kind of religion imaginable striving to experience it.

We honor it, we celebrate it, we demand it, we fight for it, we try to discover it, we pray for it. It is an overwhelming desire deep within us all. We were created to enjoy it, to experience nothing less. But in the far reaches of our history, we lost it. The freedom we knew under God became a dream engulfed by a nightmare. That God-given ability to satisfy the desires of our heart in ways that were always pleasing to our Creator became distorted and strained. But we still longed for freedom and continued attempting to find it in all the wrong places. So we became slaves—slaves to cravings that drew us further away from God, from the One who lovingly created us free to serve Him. Traces of our original dream still linger; deep within our souls we still hunger for freedom. But we'll never find it apart from God.

Death by Decision

True freedom has its critics—people who think that too much leeway will always cause a fall into immorality. Paul answers this argument against freedom by telling us that we are to consider ourselves dead to sin and alive to God through Christ. He defines death as separation from a relationship rather than the extinction of the body or the soul or the self. We are therefore to separate ourselves from the "relationship" with sin and be in communion (intimate fellowship) with God in Christ. That obviously does not mean that Christians cannot commit sins but that we no longer practice, nor are we any longer slaves to sin. But we can choose to renew that relationship by choosing to sin.

Paul also talks about our being "baptized into Christ Jesus," being "baptized into His death," and being "buried with Him through baptism into death." Let us discover more about this baptism.

Read Philippians 3:8–11; Galatians 2:19–21; Colossians 2:11–15.

Questions:

What does it mean to be baptized into the death of Jesus Christ?

✎ _____

_____

_____

How does your union with Christ in His death separate you from sin's power and bring you freedom?

✎ _____

_____

_____

In what ways can this freedom be experienced in your life?

✎ _____

_____

_____

Word Wealth—*Baptizm*

Baptizm: Greek *baptisma* (bap-tis-mah); Strong's #908: From the verb *baptize* meaning to dip or immerse. At its root it connotes being overwhelmed or wholly covered. *Baptisma* then, is the result of having been immersed, overwhelmed and utterly covered.

Kingdom Life—*Sin's Dominion Is Ended*

With our pre-Christian life crucified and sin's dominating power over our lives short-circuited, we are freed from their spiritual consequence. Our "old man" (the person we were before conversion to the kingdom, the one who lived under the unrestrained dominion of our sin nature) is overwhelmed by the powerful, saving love of Christ. Our "body of sin" (our will, emotions, mind, body—whatever is dominated by sin) has been crucified with Christ. The power of sin has been "done away with"—sin's power has been made inoperative, been defeated and deprived of power.

But sin has not become extinct nor been totally destroyed. We are no longer controlled by the love of sin or its ruling power in our lives; we are dead to its enslaving power, but not dead to all of its influence. Sin is no longer the master by default, but our right to choose remains intact. We have a continual choice, day-after-day, whether to yield ourselves to sin or to God.

Though we can never say in this life that we are free from all sin, we should never declare defeat in the face of sin's relentless temptation. The power of Christ's Resurrection at work within us is greater than the power of any sin, no matter how long established in our lives. We can die to sin, not because of the law forbidding it, but through all the resources that grace provides.

Read Romans 6:4–14; James 3:2; 1 John 1:8, 10; John 8:31–36.

Questions:

What do we mean by the "indwelling resurrection power of Christ"?

_____

_____

_____

What are the resources of grace?

_____

_____

_____

What sin continues to attempt to re-assert its hold in your life?

_____

_____

_____

How can you experience release from this temptation?

_____

_____

_____

Three Steps to Freedom

We have discovered some great truths about our new life in Christ and how we can know they are true. But how can they become realities in our daily lives? After all, we still fall prey to temptation. We still feel sin's tug even though its power does not hold sway over us as it used to. How do we deal with this? Paul tells us in verses 11–23, giving us three steps we must take so we can experience our new freedom.

Step 1—Reckon

The first step is to *reckon*. The Greek verb translated *reckon* means "to consider, to take into account." And its verb tense coupled with its meaning gives us the idea of "continually considering, constantly taking into account." There are two truths we need to keep on considering—we are dead to sin and we are alive to God. These truths are valid and operational only in and through Christ Jesus.

Questions:

What does it mean to you to be "alive to God"?

_____

_____

_____

What role does your "thought life" play in victory over sin?

_____

_____

_____

Step 2—Present

The essence of the second step is found in the Greek word translated *present*. Paul calls on us to submit ourselves to God as resurrected from sin's penalty and power to become His servants of righteous living. We don't serve sin anymore; sin is no longer our master. God is our new master, and we are His servants because of our identification and union with His Son through His crucifixion, death, burial, and resurrection. As His servants, we are called on to counter sin's advances with the good offense of godly living.

Questions:

Do you daily present yourself to God to be directed and used in His service?

✎_____

_____

_____

_____

How might your life change if you began each day consciously dedicating yourself in service to Him?

✎_____

_____

_____

_____

Step 3—Choose

The third step is choosing whom we will serve. We now belong to Christ and are members of His kingdom, but God will not override our right to choose, our free will. He wants us to serve Him out of our own desire, prompted by our love for Him. At his death, Joshua set forth a challenge, "choose for yourselves this day whom you will serve" (Joshua 24:15). His entreaty still reverberates throughout the kingdom.

Questions:

How does our right to choose play into the entire process of salvation?

✎_____

_____

_____

_____

In what way do your choices inhibit God's best in your life?

✏️_____

_____

_____

_____

Probing the Depths

Christ's program of deliverance breaks bondage to *both* our flesh (selfish desires and self-will) and the Devil's mastery. However, we may still suffer from the effect of satan's strongholds in our lives *now*. These strongholds actually exist through issues of the past. Their torment can seem alive and well, but they are only ghosts of yesterday. They are empowered only when we choose to listen to their lies.

The lies of the past can keep us in deceptive bondage; a bondage that requires our assent to be empowered. Sometimes it may seem we will never be free. But God has provided the means of deliverance. The torment will be broken as the truth makes us free!

Read 2 Corinthians 10:3–6; Philippians 4:6–8; John 8:31–36.

Questions:

Are there any past issues in your life that continually beckon you toward bondage?

✏️_____

_____

_____

_____

What action can you take to begin to experience freedom?

✏️_____

_____

_____

_____

What reasons might cause you to choose bondage to sin rather than freedom in Christ?

✎ _____

_____

_____

Kingdom Life—*The War Within*

Paul is very candid with us regarding his past sinful state "under the law" and his propensity to sin even though freed from sin's dominion by Christ's redemption.

The law of God serves as a standard against which our sinful nature is measured. It is the law that reveals sin as sin. The law forbade certain actions and, because of our sinful nature, to be forbidden creates the desire to engage in the prohibited act. Therefore, grace rescues us from the otherwise inevitable: sin leading to greater sin, leading to death.

By His grace, God enables us to be redeemed and freed from the penalty of breaking His law. Knowing we are unable to follow the law and therefore cannot be made righteous through it, God sent His Son to be made sin for us, dying our death and rising to new life so we might be partakers of new life in Him.

But sin remains, and our struggle with it continues. We know what is right and desire to do what is pleasing to God, but sin is tenacious in its hold on our lives. We find ourselves doing or desiring those things that God forbids and failing to do what we know will please Him. There is a constant battle between our sinful nature and our enlightened understanding as a new creature in Christ.

Read 2 Corinthians 4:16; Galatians 5:17, 18; James 4:1–7; 1 Peter 2:11, 12.

Questions:

In what ways do you experience this war in your own life?

✎ _____

_____

_____

How can you fight and win this war?

✎ _____

_____

_____

_____

How can we help one another find victory over the struggle with sin?

✎ _____

_____

_____

_____

Record Your Thoughts

Many find great encouragement in Paul's testimony of his apparent struggle to overcome. It's good to know we are not the only ones to ever experience the frustration in overcoming sin in our lives. Paul describes a desperate situation, an experience filled with disappointment and a sense of hopelessness. Even he cries out in despair after recounting it.

Questions:

Do you ever experience overwhelming despair over your failures to live as God desires?

✎ _____

_____

_____

_____

Have you ever given up and conceded defeat?

✎ _____

_____

_____

_____

What has God provided that will enable you to fight and win against the enemy?

✎ _____

_____

_____

_____

_____

Your Inheritance

Romans 8:1–39

✞ Kingdom Key—*We Are Heirs*

Ephesians 1:13–14 "Having believed, you were sealed with the Holy Spirit of promise, who is the guarantee of our inheritance."

You have an inheritance that is not subject to loss or the effects of fraud. It is reserved for you and watched over by your Father God (1 Peter 1:3–5). It's a legacy, a memorial, a sign of love from the One who has gone ahead of us.

Jesus Christ so loved you that He not only set you free but left you an inheritance that can never be matched, much less superseded. It's a wonderful, incredible, absolutely glorious demonstration of His infinite, unconditional love for you. This marvelous gift hinges on the Third Person of the Trinity, the Holy Spirit. The Holy Spirit's indwelling power is both the sign and seal that we are heirs of God's promise.

Read Galatians 3:26, 29; 1 Corinthians 6:9–11; Ephesians 1:13–14; Galatians 4:17; Matthew 25:34; James 2:5.

Questions:

Do you think of yourself as an heir of Almighty God?

✐ _____

_____

_____

_____

_____

At this point, what do you perceive you have inherited?

✎ _____

_____

_____

How would thinking of yourself as an heir of God change the way you relate to life?

✎ _____

_____

_____

_____

Word Wealth—*Inheritance*

Inheritance: Hebrew *cheleq* (chay-lek); Strong's #2506: A portion, part, inheritance, allotment. This noun occurs more than sixty times in the Old Testament. It comes from the verb *chalaq*, "to be smooth." From this root are derived such words as "smooth stones" and "flattery," which is smooth words. Perhaps because smooth stones were used for casting "lots," *chalaq* came to mean "to apportion, deal out, divide up, allot." Thus a *cheleq* is an apportionment, allotment, a parcel of land that a person receives as an inheritance.

The Holy Spirit Brings Victory

Toward the end of Romans 7, Paul almost ended on a note of despair. How could he possibly fight and win the war raging within him between the old man dominated by sin and the new man hooked on good? It is only "through Jesus Christ our Lord" that Paul or any believer has a fighting chance. Christ brings the Holy Spirit to enable us to fight and win the war within. Apart from the Holy Spirit's work in our lives, it would be utterly impossible for anyone to live the Christian life, because only God's Spirit makes such a life possible through His enabling power and other resources. Without the Holy Spirit, sin would continue to have the upper hand in our lives.

Read Romans 8:1–4.

Questions:

What has set us free from God's condemnation?

✎ _____

_____

_____

_____

What should be the result of this freedom in your day-to-day life?

✎ _____

_____

_____

_____

Do you ever feel condemned by God?

✎ _____

_____

_____

_____

What can and should be your reaction?

✎ _____

_____

_____

_____

Through the atoning work of Christ, Christians are free from God's banishing judgment; we are no longer condemned under the law. Knowing we are no longer condemned and feeling as if that's true can sometimes be two very different things. If you are a believer and ever feel like you're under the condemning hand of God, you need to ignore your feelings and let the truth of your relationship with Him take hold. Commit Romans 8:1 to memory or write it on cards and stick them in several places where you will see them often. Let this truth penetrate to the depths of your being. It will refresh your soul and transform your feelings.

The new life we live in Christ requires a new way of thinking and a Christ-centered focus of attention.

Too often we act as though our thought life is somehow disconnected from our area of responsibility. We tend to treat it as though it is something that happens to us over which we have no control. (It's the circumstance that is causing the negative thoughts, or it's what someone else has said or done that is making our thoughts poisonous.) We act as though we are victims of our own thoughts and have no power to direct them. When we do this, we buy into a lie that has limitless power to destroy. We literally think ourselves into defeat because we do not take responsibility for where we allow our minds to travel.

But we have the right and the responsibility to think on those things which bring light and life. We can behave as the victim of our own thoughts, blaming everything but ourselves, or we can bring every thought captive, purposing in our hearts to center our minds on the things of the Lord. We must accept the responsibility and determine that we will bring our every thought into line with the Word of God. We can literally choose thoughts of darkness or thoughts of light. We can choose to entertain words of life or meditate on words of death.

Read Romans 8:5–7; Philippians 4:8; 2 Corinthians 10:4–5; Proverbs 23:7.

Questions:

Have you ever truly paid attention to the thoughts that wander unchecked through your mind?

How might "taking them captive" change the way you live and relate to others?

✎ _____

_____

_____

_____

The Deeds of the Body

There are two distinct directions for life and each has its own predetermined consequences. Paul tells us that, though we are Christians, we can choose to live carnally (according to the dictates of our sinful nature). A carnal life can never please God; but if we employ the power granted to us by the indwelling of the Holy Spirit, we can cease to walk in sinful ways. This ability to choose and the practice of doing so is a good summary of the process of sanctification (growth in holiness) in the Christian life. We are to actively work at growing in holiness and "putting to death" any sin in our hearts or minds, as well as in our words and deeds. Yet, in spite of the fact that we actively put forth effort, Paul reminds us that it is only by the Holy Spirit's power that we can succeed.

Read Romans 8:12–14; James 2:14–25.

Questions:

What does it mean to be debtors to the Spirit?

✎ _____

_____

_____

Have you made a practice of choosing to operate in the Holy Spirit's power in your life?

✎ _____

_____

How can you improve this in the future?

✎ _____

_____

_____

In looking back at your walk with the Lord, what progress do you see toward sanctification?

✎ _____

_____

_____

Probing the Depths

Now take your understanding of "put to death the deeds of the body" and commit to turning to the Holy Spirit daily, petitioning Him to inform you about how to do this and then to enable you to follow through.

Remember, this is a prayer request the Spirit will always answer because it clearly accords with God's will. So if you ever fall prey to the deeds of your sin nature, don't blame that on the Spirit. He will always meet your need in this area. Any failures you experience will be your responsibility, not His.

Led by the Spirit

"For, as many as are led by the Spirit of God, these are the sons of God." This verse at Romans 8:14 is more than a synonym for Christians. It describes the life-style of those who are "sons of God." Paul is giving encouragement not to live according to the flesh, but to put to death the deeds of the body. Therefore, being "led by the Spirit of God" involves progressively putting to death the sinful appetites of our sin nature. This implies that, while all Christians are in some general sense being "led by the Spirit of God," there are increasing degrees of being led by the Spirit. The more fully people are led by the Holy Spirit, the more completely will they be obedient to God and be conformed to His holy standards.

The sense of the word *led* as translated in Romans 8:14 is one of continuing action. Therefore, this verse may be translated "as many as are continually being led by the Spirit of God." This leading is not to be restricted to knowledge of the commands of Scripture and conscious effort to obey them (though it most certainly includes that). Rather, it more fully includes being sensitive to the promptings of the Holy Spirit throughout the day, promptings that, if genuinely from the Holy Spirit, will never encourage us to act contrary to Scripture.

Questions:

Do you often "hear" the Holy Spirit directing you?

_____

_____

_____

_____

What ways can you be sure you are actually hearing from God?

_____

_____

_____

_____

Will the Holy Spirit ever speak or direct you in things that are contrary to the Word of God?

_____

_____

_____

_____

Word Wealth—*Abba*

Abba: Aramaic [AB ah] *(father)*—corresponds to the English "Daddy" or "Papa." It occurs three times in the New Testament: in Jesus' prayer amid His struggle in the Garden of Gethsemane (Mark 14:36); and twice in Paul's words describing the believer's intimacy with God through the "Spirit of adoption."

Kingdom Life—*We Are Heirs of Promise*

You have been adopted. You are a beloved child of the one true God! Just as a loving, earthly father dotes on his child, so your heavenly Father dotes on you. Just as a loved and treasured child runs to his father yelling "Daddy!" so you can joyfully run to your heavenly Father crying "Abba, Father!" He chose you, He loves you and His arms ever wait to enfold you.

Because of this love, God has made you His heir. When Christ died, being both fully God and fully man, He left to all God's children all He possessed as the Second Person of the Trinity. This is your spiritual inheritance.

The biblical concept of a spiritual inheritance for believers is primarily of Jewish origin. But the analogy used to reveal this concept was adapted to and influenced by Greek and Roman inheritance practices. Three of these influences were: (1) inheritance was regarded as immediate as well as ultimate, (2) all legitimate heirs usually shared the inheritance equally and jointly rather than a division favoring a firstborn son, and (3) legally adopted children enjoyed full inheritance rights along with natural offspring.

The Christian's spiritual inheritance is based strictly on our relationship to Christ. This spiritual birthright cannot be inherited by those who do not know and serve God. The present possession of the spiritual inheritance as well as its future glory is emphasized in Romans 8: "The Spirit Himself bears witness with our spirit that we are the children of God, and if children, then heirs—heirs of God and joint heirs with Christ, if indeed we suffer with Him, that we may also be glorified together" (Romans 8:16–17).

The Holy Spirit's indwelling power is both the sign and seal that we are heirs of God's promise. Those who are redeemed become God's adopted sons with full inheritance rights.

Read Galatians 3:26, 29; 1 Corinthians 6:9–11; Ephesians 1:13–14; Galatians 4:17.

Questions:

In your life now, what are ways in which you experience being an heir of God?

✎ _____

_____

_____

_____

How might recognition of the degree of God's love for you change the way you live?

✎ _____

_____

_____

_____

We Suffer with Christ

Suffering is a fact of the Christian walk. This is not something we like to hear. Yet we are told throughout the New Testament that suffering various trials, tribulations and persecutions is to be expected, even welcomed by those whom God is perfecting, changing from the inside out.

Paul shows us that sufferings are vastly different issues than mere temporary difficulty or pain. The whole scope of spiritual warfare, persecution, and oppression is in focus.

Read Matthew 5:11, 12; Mark 8:34–38; John 15:18–21; 16:33; Acts 14:21; 1 Peter 3:13–17; 4:12–19; James 1:2–4.

Questions:

What is your response to trial in your life?

✎ _____

_____

_____

_____

How can you be changed by experiencing trial?

✎ _____

_____

_____

How does realizing you are suffering with Christ, change the way you view trials?

✎ _____

_____

_____

What spiritual tools have you been given to enable you to walk through trials as a child of the kingdom?

✎ _____

_____

_____

 Kingdom Life—*Trust God*

Even in hardship and suffering, even in bitter disappointment, even when wrongly treated, Christians can know that God will work amidst such situations to fulfill His purpose in His children—always for their good. The situation may or may not be directly changed by God, but even if situations stay difficult God guarantees ultimate good results, including maturation of character in His children.

You can trust your Father. His love for you is assured, regardless of the circumstance. You can rest securely in that love and know He will only work for your good. Whether a circumstance is instituted by God or allowed by Him, it first passes through His hand before it touches your life. You can trust in His love and know you are safe.

Read Hebrews 12:3–11.

Questions:

Have you ever become "weary and discouraged" as a result of circumstances?

✎ _____

_____

_____

Trials teach. What have you learned through trial that you could not have learned any other way?

✎ _____

_____

_____

In what way can trials be considered an honor bestowed by the Lord?

✎ _____

_____

_____

Word Wealth—*Foreknew/Predistined/Called/ Justified/Glorified*

Foreknew (v. 29): The aspect of God's omniscience whereby He knows the future of all things and events before they ever come to be.

Predestined (v. 29): The act of God's will whereby He determines what will take place and how it will occur, whether through His free will or His permission of the free will of others.

Called (v. 30): God's invitation to come to Him by faith.

Justified (v. 30): The act of God whereby He declares believing sinners righteous and as now without a record of past sin.

Glorified (v. 30): Our future state of heavenly perfection and bliss; our ultimate inheritance. It's the promised culmination of the sanctification process begun after we place our faith in Christ. And it's so certain that Paul can refer to it in the past tense.

More Than Conquerors

We have been given a promise, a guarantee from God Almighty. We have every reason to have unshakable security regardless of our present trials. Our future destiny is predetermined and absolute.

We are as secure as secure can be—now and forever. The God of the entire universe—the greatest power and lover of all—gives us His perfect guarantee, and He is never wrong and He cannot lie (Titus 1:2).

Word Wealth—*More Than Conquerors*

More Than Conquerors; Greek *hupernikao* (hoo-er-nik-ah′-oh); Strong's #5245: From *huper*, which means "over and above," and *nikao*, meaning "to conquer."

The word describes one who is super victorious, who wins more than an ordinary victory, but who is overpowering in achieving abundant victory. This is not the language of conceit, but of confidence. Christ's love conquered death, and because of His love, we are hupernikao!!

Record Your Thoughts

Questions:

How have you responded to trial and difficult circumstances in the past?

✎ _____

_____

_____

_____

How has this study changed your view of suffering?

✎ _____

_____

_____

_____

How can you take this from merely "head knowledge" into heart experience?

✎ _____

_____

_____

_____

What role do those brothers and sisters in the Lord, whom the Lord has put in your life, play in your ability to walk as "more than a conqueror"?

_____

_____

_____

_____

_____

ADDITIONAL OBSERVATIONS

SESSION EIGHT

God's Faithfullness

Romans 9:1—11:36

1 Thessalonians 5:24 "He who calls you is faithful, who also will do it."

How many times has someone promised to do something for you, only to let you down? Broken promises create anxiety, anger, guilt, frustration, and disappointment. Nowhere is this more clearly seen than in a person's relationship to God.

Feeling that God has broken His promise can create feelings of bitterness, hostility, and the desire for revenge. It can even cause us to doubt that we are redeemed and sometimes even cause us to question God's existence.

Have you ever felt that toward God? Have you ever believed that He let you down—that His promises meant nothing, that He was only playing with your mind and emotions, that He never intended to follow through on what He said He would do? If so, you're not alone. At various times in human history, even some of the men and women in Scripture doubted God's promises.

Read Genesis 18:9–15; Job 16:6–17; Luke 1:18–20.

But if Scripture records anything, it records hundreds upon hundreds of instances where God promised to do something and then did it. So unfailingly consistent has He been that the biblical writers remark about it frequently, even referring to the Lord as the One who is ever faithful, even when we are not. Only God always keeps His promises, but somehow, this doesn't stop us from doubting Him.

Read Psalm 119:89–91; Hosea 11:12; 1 Thessalonians 5:24; 2 Timothy 2:13.

Questions:

Have you ever felt that God broke His word to you?

_____

_____

_____

_____

What were the resulting emotions?

_____

_____

_____

_____

How did you find your way out of the emotional storm?

_____

_____

_____

_____

Looking back, can you see a reason for the situation?

_____

_____

_____

_____

Word Wealth—*Israelites/Adoption/Glory/Covenants/ Law/Service/Promises/Fathers*

In order to clarify Romans 9, take a look at the following terms and their definitions. Remember that Israel is God's chosen people.

Israelites (v. 4): The descendants of Jacob, who had been renamed Israel (Genesis 32:28). Designations such as "Israel" and "Israelites" conveyed to Jews that they were God's chosen people.

Adoption (v. 4): This term refers to God's adoption of the nation of Israel as His son (Exodus 4:22, 23; Jeremiah 31:9; Hosea 11:1).

Glory (v. 4): The majestic manifestation of God's presence, which, during Israel's history, often occurred in the form of a radiant, almost blinding cloud (Exodus 16:7, 10; 40:34–38; Ezekiel 1:28).

Covenants (v. 4): Pacts or treaties God made with individuals (such as Abraham, Genesis 15:1–21, and David, 2 Samuel 23:5) and the nation of Israel (Exodus 19:5; 24:1–8).

Law (v. 4): The set of instructions God gave the nation of Israel through Moses (Exodus).

Service (v. 4): The instructions God gave to Moses concerning Israel's worship of Him (Leviticus; see also Hebrews 9:1–6).

Promises (v. 4): The hundreds of promises God made to Israel throughout the Old Testament (see also Acts 13:29–39; Ephesians 2:12).

Fathers (v. 5): Sometimes called *patriarchs*, these are Abraham, Isaac, Jacob, Jacob's twelve sons, and other notables in Israel's history, such as David (Mark 11:10; Acts 2:29).

Behind the Scenes

An often misunderstood concept is God's choice of one person rather than another, such as with Isaac and Ishmael, and Jacob and Esau. Neither example concerns the salvation of these individuals, but both involve God's making a choice among the physical descendants of Abraham for the establishment of the spiritual line of promise. God declared that the Messiah would come through Isaac's line (Genesis 21:12). God also made a sovereign choice between Jacob and Esau, electing Jacob as the one through whom the messianic line would continue (Genesis 25:23).

When the text says that God loved Jacob but hated Esau, it does not mean that God cared for one and despised the other. Rather, the love-hate idea concerns God's choice of one twin over the other to carry on the physical line of the Messiah; it has nothing to do with His commitment to or feelings toward either person (see Matthew 6:24; Luke 14:26; John 12:25). God loves all human beings and desires only their best, if they will but choose Him by faith (John 3:16–18; 1 Timothy 2:3–6). Jacob and Esau, and Isaac and Ishmael all had the very real opportunity to freely accept or reject a faith-relationship with the Lord. Read Acts 10:34–43.

Questions:

Have you ever felt you were left out of God's plan and promises?

_____

_____

_____

Have you ever felt like you were an "Esau" to God?

_____

_____

_____

How has this affected your life?

_____

_____

_____

How do you now perceive those feelings?

_____

_____

_____

God Is Always Just

With God's willingness and sovereignty to choose firmly demonstrated from Israel's history, Paul considers the objection that such action on God's part leads to the conclusion that He is unjust (Romans 9:14). Paul appeals to the Old Testament story about Moses and Pharaoh and the Exodus of the Israelites from Egypt (vv. 15–18) to show that God has every right to show mercy to whomever He wants.

God's chosen people are enslaved in Egypt. He hears their cries for help and enlists Moses to act as His spokesman before Pharaoh, the ruler of Egypt. Before Moses goes in front of Pharaoh, however, God tells him that Pharaoh will not let the Israelites leave willingly. He says that He will harden Pharaoh's heart so that he will put up a fight and refuse to grant Moses' request to release the Israelites. The reason is found in the words Moses spoke to Pharaoh: "For this very purpose I have raised you [Pharaoh] up, that I may show My power in you, and that My name may be declared in all the earth" (Exodus 9:16). The rest is history. Pharaoh might have been a gracious liberator, but he chose to be a hateful one. He did eventually release the Israelites, but not until some incredible miracles had occurred in Egypt—supernatural events that convinced both the Egyptians and the Israelites that the God of the Israelites was Lord over all.

The issue of personal salvation is *not* in view here. Paul is making a case for God's right to choose and that His choice is always just. Salvation from everlasting death to everlasting life has *not* been the focus in his examples.

Questions:

Have you ever felt "unjustly" treated by God?

_____

_____

_____

_____

What part might your attitudes have played in the circumstances and their outcome?

_____

_____

_____

Word Wealth—*Mercy/Hardens*

Mercy (v. 15): Going beyond justice to give a person what is not deserved or to restrain from giving a person what is deserved; showing kindness and concern for someone in serious need.

Hardens (v. 18): Since this Greek word translated *hardens* refers to the Hebrew words used for *harden* in Exodus, we need to look back to the Hebrew terms to understand what Paul means.

The three Hebrew words translated *hardened* in the Exodus account of Pharaoh's hardening his heart have similar meanings. The word most frequently used means "to make strong, to strengthen, to harden" (Exodus 4:21; 7:13, 22; 8:19; 9:12, 35; 10:20, 27; 11:10; 14:4, 8, 17). The next most commonly used word (which is translated once as *stubborn*, Exodus 7:14) means "dullness" or "insensitivity" (Exodus 8:15, 32; 9:7, 34; 10:1). The third Hebrew term occurs once (Exodus 7:3), and it means "stubborn, stiff-necked."

When considered together and in their various contexts, none of these words carry the idea of someone being forced to do something against his or her will. Instead, these terms convey the idea that Pharaoh was made more tenacious in his own already chosen path of pride and rebellion.

 Kingdom Extra—*The Conundrum of Sovereignty and Free Will*

Fewer topics create more controversy than the subject of the relationship between divine sovereignty and human freedom. Some people emphasize God's sovereignty to the exclusion of human freedom. Others downplay God's sovereignty and exalt human freedom. Many people just throw up their hands, claiming that the issue is absolutely impossible to resolve because it contradicts reason.

If you would like to dig deeper into this whole discussion, the books below will help you wade through the labyrinth while presenting a number of different positions.

Basinger, David, and Randall Basinger. *Predestination and Free Will: Four Views of Divine Sovereignty and Human Freedom*. Downers Grove, IL: InterVarsity Press, 1986.

Billheimer, Paul E. *The Mystery of God's Providence*. Wheaton, IL: Tyndale House, 1983.

Craig, William Lane. *The Only Wise God: The Compatibility of Divine Foreknowledge and Human Freedom*. Grand Rapids, MI: Baker Book House, 1987.

Fisk, Samuel. *Divine Sovereignty and Human Freedom*. Neptune, NJ: Loizeaux Brothers, 1973.

Forster, Roger T., and V. Paul Marston. *God's Strategy in Human History.* Wheaton, IL: Tyndale House, 1973.

Packer, J. I. *Evangelism and the Sovereignty of God.* Downers Grove, IL: InterVarsity Press, 1961.

Pinnock, Clark H., ed. *The Grace of God, the Will of Man.* Grand Rapids, MI: Zondervan Publishing House, 1989.

Grace Unlimited. Minneapolis, MN: Bethany Fellowship, 1975.

Rupp, E. Gordon, and Philip S. Watson, eds. *Luther and Erasmus: Free Will and Salvation.* Philadelphia, PA: Westminster Press, 1969.

Shank, Robert. *Elect in the Son.* Minneapolis, MN: Bethany House, 1989.

Above All

In the final four verses of Romans 11, Paul launches into a doxology—a fitting way to end some of the most incredible truths regarding God's ways in human history. In this outburst of praise, Paul enumerates the characteristics of God with which he is familiar. Read them and, with each, ask yourself if you know God in that way. If not, ask Him to teach you His nature more fully. What an incredible journey awaits those who will seek God with all their heart, with all their mind, with all their strength.

Record Your Thoughts

Questions:

Do you believe that God loves you and only wants the best for you?

_____

_____

_____

_____

Does that belief show in the way you respond to trials?

_____

_____

_____

_____

How can this affect the way you relate to the people in your life?

_____

_____

_____

_____

What are God's promises to you?

_____

_____

_____

_____

A Transformed Life

Romans 12:1–21

✝ Kingdom Key—*We Are Being Changed*

2 Corinthians 3:18 "But we all, with unveiled face, beholding as in a mirror the glory of the Lord, are being transformed into the same image from glory to glory, just as by the Spirit of the Lord."

The voice of the world says, "Me first." Paul tells us to give ourselves over as "a living sacrifice" to God and others. Greater opposites never existed.

Serving self first will never bring lasting happiness. Sure, it may feel good for the short haul. In fact, you may even feel as if you deserve to have your needs and wants met above those of others. But if you really live with self-service as your maxim, you will miss genuine, lasting joy. You will miss the Christian life and all the blessings that come with it because the life we are to live through Christ begins with other-service, which is just another name for self-sacrifice.

This is transformed sacrificial living. It changes our character, our minds, our hearts, until our most basic drive in life is to help others, to serve them in every way we can so they too will not only see but desire and even begin to live and enjoy the life of other-centered living in Christ.

It seems so backward, so contrary to the way our society wants us to live. We think our viewpoint is normal, but it isn't, not for children of the kingdom. Our perspective is messed up, confused, irrational. God's is perfect, clear, and eminently rational. So if you have to, work through this lesson standing on your head—intellectually and practically, that is. Paul is about to reorient our thinking so it resembles God's.

Read Matthew 20:25–28; Galatians 5:13–14; John 15:13–17.

Questions:

In what ways does the "me first" attitude show up in your life?

✎ _____

_____

_____

_____

In your opinion, what does sacrificial servanthood look like?

✎ _____

_____

_____

_____

Word Wealth—*Sacrifice*

Sacrifice: Hebrew *thusia* (thoo-see'-ah); Strong's #2378: the act of offering something precious to God; to kill, usually by fire. The destruction or surrender of something for the sake of something else; a giving over of legitimate claim.

Kingdom Life—*A Living Sacrifice*

Since Christians are the new people of God, the "New Israel," then should we not offer sacrifices to God, just as the Old Testament Jews did? Yes, but not animal sacrifices at the temple in Jerusalem; rather we should offer our bodies (all that we are) as "living sacrifices" each day to God.

Jesus taught that to be of value in the kingdom of God, one must be a servant. A servant does not have the option of putting himself first. A servant's purpose is to provide what is needed or requested by the one he serves. We are to surrender our time, our desires, all that we have and are to the service of our Lord. We are to be consecrated, set apart to His service. We are his body on earth so He will direct us to do as He did: give our lives in service to others.

Read Luke 10:30–37; 1 Corinthians 13:3.

Questions:

Do you make it a practice to serve others even when it is inconvenient?

_____

_____

_____

_____

What part does love play in giving your self as "a living sacrifice"?

_____

_____

_____

_____

How might this result in the keeping of all the commandments?

_____

_____

_____

_____

Kingdom Life—*Set Apart for Service*

To be consecrated is to be dedicated or set apart for God's use. In the Old Testament, those things and people that were to be used in service to God were anointed, consecrated, and counted as holy to the Lord. We have been "anointed" by the blood of Christ and set apart from all else as holy. The children of the kingdom are to be consecrated to the Lord's service. This means that serving God and the people of God is the main work in the life of a Christian.

You have been anointed and your primary objective and purpose should now be to be used by God in whatever way He chooses. You are to be a tool of righteousness in the hand of the Almighty, bringing His light and life through Jesus Christ to all your life touches.

Read Matthew 5:14–16.

Questions:

Do you think of yourself as holy to the Lord?

_____

_____

_____

What difference would full realization of this make in your attitudes and actions?

_____

_____

_____

What hinders you from making service your primary objective?

_____

_____

_____

Word Wealth—*Conform/Transformed*

Conform: Greek *suschematizo* (soos-khay´-mat-id´-zo); Strong's #4964: refers to conforming oneself to the outer fashion or outward appearance, accommodating oneself to a model or matter. *Suschematizo* occurs only one other time in the New Testament at 1 Peter 1:14, where it describes those conforming themselves to worldly lusts. Even apparent or superficial conformity to the present world system or any accommodation to its ways could be fatal to the Christian walk.

Transformed: Greek *metamorphoo* (met-am-or-fo´-o); Strong's #3339; a metamorphosis; a complete change in nature and form. This word denotes becoming something entirely different and new. It is to be reformed, altered completely from what once was.

Kingdom Extra

What impact does the way we think, what things we ponder, what opinions and judgments we entertain, have on our ability to walk effectively and productively with the Lord?

To "renew" is "to renovate," implying a restoration to an original state. It intimates the potential of redemption's power to reinstate features of God's original intention for humanity as designed before the Fall. The "mind" constitutes the intellect or understanding, but also includes all that is described in the word "mind-set," that is, the feelings and the will.

Below you will find a paraphrase of Romans 12:1–2. It is not meant as an exact translation, but a restating in familiar words to enable a fuller understanding.

I absolutely implore you! I even beg you! In light of God's ultimate compassion for you, make a conscious choice to yield to Him. Command your thoughts and emotions to come into line with His Spirit within you, to come into agreement with His plan for your life. Give up your rights to and your claim upon your past pain, present experience and future hope. Give them into His hand that you may become a channel through which His righteousness can be manifested. What other choice is there if we truly recognize who He is? If we truly believe He is Almighty, the great I AM?

Resist thinking like the world and reacting in the ways you did when you were of the world. Rather, set out to change your ways of thinking. Your perceptions and understanding must be made entirely new. Your thoughts and feelings must be recognized as of the world and you must choose a new alignment. Consciously align yourself with the revealed will of God. You must consciously choose to surrender to the Spirit in order to be brought to the place where you can experience a way of thinking that is in complete agreement with the will of God. By choosing to allow the Lord to renew your mind you will be freed to exhibit to the world the perfect will of God.

Read Proverbs 23:7; Ephesians 4:17–24; 2 Corinthians 10:4–6.

In 2 Corinthians 10:4–5, Paul refers specifically to warfare in the mind, against arrogant, rebellious ideas and attitudes (which he terms arguments), and against every high thing (pride) opposed to the true knowledge of God. The aim is to bring every disobedient thought into obedience (attentive hearing, listening with compliant submission, assent and agreement) to Christ. Strongholds, places of sin and darkness within, are first established in the mind. That is why we are to take every thought captive, and submit to the working of the Lord, the prompting of the Holy Spirit, to renew our minds.

Questions:

In what ways do your thoughts defeat you?

_____

_____

_____

_____

If you refuse to allow your mind to dwell on the things of the world, what effect could that choice have on your walk with the Lord?

_____

_____

_____

What effect would this have on your relationship with others?

_____

_____

_____

_____

How would it change your values and priorities?

_____

_____

_____

_____

The Lure of the World

The world can look mighty appealing; it glitters tantalizingly before us each day. But we are to recognize the deceitfulness of the temporal riches and set our sights on our eternal treasure.

Read Matthew 13:22; Galatians 1:4; 1 Peter 1:14; 1 John 2:15–17.

Questions:

How are we to relate to the allure of the world?

✎_____

_____

_____

Do you find you are successful in resisting worldly attraction?

✎_____

_____

_____

What things of the world are most captivating to you?

✎_____

_____

_____

_____

How are you hindered by this?

✎_____

_____

_____

_____

Kingdom Life—*When God Calls, He Enables*

Consecration, nonconformity, transformation, evaluation (verse 3)—these are all acts of individuals looking inward, assessing and redirecting themselves in the power of God's Spirit toward a godly character, perspective, and life-style. Once we are actively engaged there, however, we will have to move outward, toward serving others. The Christian life was never meant to be lived apart from community. We are not loners for Christ—rugged individualists looking out only for ourselves. Any self-directed work must eventually turn to other-directed work. Just as Christ came to save and serve others, so He calls on us, His adopted children, to reach out to others with His salvation message and to help them grow up in the family of faith.

Now God doesn't just call us to service and then leave us on our own. He never leaves us in the lurch. Whatever He calls us to do, He also equips us to do. God gives us the gifts and the faith we need to use those gifts.

Read 1 Corinthians 12:4–26.

Questions:

Do you experience the unity and connectedness that should be experienced from being in the body of Christ?

_____

_____

_____

Do you use the gifts God has given you to serve others?

_____

_____

_____

How are these two things connected; how does one affect the other?

_____

_____

_____

Kingdom Extra

For a greater understanding of the gifts listed in Romans 12:6–8, you may wish to locate a copy of the *People of the Spirit Participants Guide*. You may also employ the aid of a Bible commentary and dictionary. A brief explanation may be found in the *New Spirit-Filled Life Study Bible* footnote entries for these verses.

An Alien Lifestyle

At the heart of transformed sacrificial living is love. In fact, without love, that kind of living is impossible. Although the word *love* does not appear throughout verses 9–21, love is definitely the guiding principle, the beacon that illuminates and directs our personal lives as well as our relationships with fellow Christians and with our adversaries.

To the world, those whose lives are transformed to the kingdom's standards seem like beings from another planet. They wonder why we would repay evil committed against us with good or serve others more than ourselves or pass up the world's allurements for some intangible joys. Once we remember that this world is fallen, so it cannot stand as the rule for what's right and reasonable, and once we recall that only God is the perfect, unchanging standard for what's good and rational, then those who follow His way are the ones to look to for what makes sense.

Following the crowd, conforming yourself to what everyone else is doing is easy. But it's also destructive. God has a much better, more sane track to follow. It's difficult, but He will always give you what you need to live life His way.

Behind the Scenes

Verse 20 requires some explanation. At first blush, the verse appears to present a backhanded way we can get revenge against our enemies. All we have to do, the verse seems to say, is be especially nice to them, and in turn our actions will increase the level of the condemnation our enemies will experience at the hands of God. If verse 20 really taught this, it would contradict the spirit of the verse's entire context. Rather, providing an opportunity for our enemies to repent and find forgiveness is what this verse is conveying. In other words, by returning evil with good, evil can be conquered rather than perpetuated by acts of vengeance. After all, what better way to conquer evil than by loving evildoers so much that they turn from evil and commit themselves to good? Isn't that what God the Father is seeking to do through His supreme act of sacrifice and love—the giving of His Son on our behalf, even to the point of crucifixion?

Record Your Thoughts

Questions:

How does your thought life affect your service to God and others?

✎ _____

_____

_____

In reading Romans 12:9–18, which of the acts of love described do you struggle with most?

_____

_____

_____

_____

What portion of this chapter most impacted you and why?

_____

_____

_____

_____

The Way of Love
Romans 13:1—15:13

Kingdom Key—We Are Aliens?

Philippians 3:20 "For our citizenship is in heaven, from which we also eagerly wait for the Savior, the Lord Jesus Christ, who will transform our lowly body that it may be conformed to His glorious body, according to the working by which He is able even to subdue all things to Himself."

Our ultimate citizenship has nothing to do with human affairs, national allegiance, or cultural heritage. We who have been born again have been translated into a higher citizenship. We live in a land that is not our own, for our inheritance is the kingdom of God.

Kingdom Life—*Translated but Not Departed*

In Romans 13:1-7 Paul exhorts his readers to fulfill their duties to the state because the authorities that exist are appointed by God. Obedience to these human authorities should be observed whether a penalty for disobedience exists or not. We obey because God established government, gave authority into their hands and commands us to obey.

Paul does not suggest that God approves a corrupt government, ungodly official, or unjust legislation. However, throughout biblical history, God allowed evil rulers to have authority for a time in order to bring about His purposes in the lives of His people. Obedience to earthly authority is the general rule we are to follow. However, loyalty to God always takes precedence over human authority. We are never to follow human authority into sin against the law or principles of

God. We are first and foremost, citizens of the kingdom and answerable to God above all.

Read Daniel 3:12–18, 4:32; Psalm 75:6, 7; Esther 4:16; Matthew 2:12; Acts 5:29; Hebrews 11:23; 1 Timothy 2:1–3.

Questions:

What is your attitude toward governmental officials with whom you disagree?

_____

_____

_____

Is political activism an acceptable course for Christians?

_____

_____

How can Christians be a light in the world of politics and government?

_____

_____

_____

_____

Love Fulfills the Law

Love is a summary of God's moral laws. It is the one characteristic that should permeate all our relationships. If we truly understood and completely followed the command to love one another, we would fulfill every social duty and would especially observe those commandments that are most fundamental in human relationships.

Whether inside or outside the body of Christ, whether in business, government or friendship, all those with whom we relate should see within us the fruit of the Holy Spirit in action: love, joy, peace, long-suffering, kindness, goodness, faithfulness, gentleness and self-control—and the greatest of these is love.

We are called to a high standard of moral conduct. We are the body of Christ in the world and the world will know Him through what it sees in us. We must submit to His lordship and accept His moral standards. To do so, we must be in constant fellowship with Him and depend on His strength and the work of the Holy Spirit within.

Read Matthew 7:12; John 13:34–35; Galatians 5:14; 1 John 4:18–19.

Questions:

How does your attitude toward government reflect the Lord?

_____

_____

_____

How is the love of Christ apparent in your business dealings?

_____

_____

_____

Does your behavior toward others change inside the church doors? Why?

_____

_____

_____

How would living in the expectation of Christ's return change your attitudes and actions?

_____

_____

_____

Love Liberates

Read Romans 14:1—15:13.

With as much as Christians agree upon, it's absolutely amazing to see how much we can find to argue about; arguments that can split friendships, and even churches. Unfortunately, this fact is nothing new; it has been with the church since its inception. But God gave His people a way to handle these matters so they wouldn't become divisive. His plan is liberating love.

Among Christians there is room for toleration and differences of opinion regarding issues that are neither commanded nor forbidden in Scripture. When any action left to personal choice is performed to honor the Lord, it is acceptable to the Lord. Christians should not judge one another with reference to the practice of these morally neutral issues. We are freed to follow the direction of the Holy Spirit in these matters and, in the final analysis, we are each responsible to God for our own actions. We will stand before Him and He will pass the final verdict.

Questions:

Are there any of these morally neutral issues over which you bear offense against others?

✎ _____

_____

_____

In light of Paul's words to the Romans, how should you handle this disagreement?

✎ _____

_____

_____

Kingdom Life—*Walk in Unity*

Christ is the model of conduct in relationships between Christians, regardless of their maturity or scruples. His example demands mutual forbearance and love. Love cannot be withheld based on differing opinions, but must be given freely. We must follow the example of our Lord and love even those who stand in opposition to us.

There is incredible power released when the body of Christ lives in unity. God's presence, power and purpose are released and unhindered in a united church—a church that operates with one accord, in like mind. As God's people, we are empowered when we cease to strive with one another and join in a unity of harmonious praise.

Read Romans 14:19; Psalm 133; Ephesians 4:1–3; 2 Chronicles 5:13, 14; Acts 2:1–4; 2 Corinthians 11:2; Revelation 21:2, 3, 9.

Questions:

How have your actions and/or attitudes hindered unity in the body of Christ?

_____

_____

_____

_____

What actions would the Lord ask of you to bring reconciliation?

_____

_____

_____

_____

How can you be used to bring peace, unity and healing into divisions in the body of Christ?

_____

_____

_____

_____

What makes the prayer in verse 13 an apt ending to this whole discussion on divisiveness and unity in the body of Christ?

_____

_____

_____

Word Wealth—*Edify*

Edify: Greek *oikodome* (oy-kod-om-ay'); Strong's #3619: to strengthen, up-hold, or build up another through patient effort, teaching and prayer; specifically within the family of God. This word has at its root the idea of building a strong structure to the glory of God.

Probing the Depths

In Scripture, the up-building of the people of God is often likened to the building of a structure. There are many similarities and many things we can learn about how to be strengthened and secure through these analogies.

Using a concordance, locate all the passages of Scripture in which a structure is in some way used as an object lesson in regard to our faith. Make a record of all that you find and ask the Lord to reveal to you any weakness in the structure of your own house of faith.

Record Your Thoughts

Questions:

At this point in your journey through Romans, what truth most impacted you?

✎_____

_____

_____

_____

Why do you suppose God is bringing this aspect of your walk with Him to the forefront?

✎_____

_____

_____

_____

In what ways have you failed to "edify" those around you?

_____

_____

_____

_____

How has this adversely affected your walk with the Lord?

_____

_____

_____

_____

ADDITIONAL OBSERVATIONS

Keep Moving On
Romans 15:14—16:27

Kingdom Key—*Maintain a Sure Focus*

Philippians 3:13–14 "Brethren, I do not count myself to have apprehended; but one thing I do, forgetting those things which are behind and reaching forward to those things which are ahead, I press toward the goal for the prize of the upward call of God in Christ Jesus."

As Paul comes to the end of his long letter to the believers in Rome, he tells them about his upcoming travel plans. Despite the hardships of travel, Paul is ready to hit the road again, but he wants the Roman Christians to know why, to understand what God has accomplished through him, and to solicit their support. But we can learn much more than simply Paul's travel plans in these last few verses of Romans.

Paul's focus remained on the purpose of God in his life. He never strayed from the path God had ordained for him to walk. What he says in these few verses speaks volumes to us—to our motivations, our ministries, our willingness to sacrifice, our values—about our own journey.

Know Whom and What You Are

Paul is probably the greatest missionary in church history. He knew he had accomplished a lot, but he was careful to say to whom the credit was due. Even as he rode on the crest of his success, humility never left his side.

He also had no trouble articulating his ministry focus. He had no doubt about what God had called him to do. He never wavered and never turned aside from the call of God. In the midst of incredible adversity, through persecution and disaster, he maintained his single focus—salvation is available to all people through Jesus Christ.

We may or may not be aware of a particular function in the body of Christ which we are called by God to fulfill. Whether we can label our function or not, we are all called to the same overriding mission as was Paul; we are to "go" and "tell." Whether in word or deed, we need to always be aware that we are the "living gospel" to an unbelieving world.

Read Mark 16:15; Matthew 5:15; 1 Peter 5:5–11.

Questions:

Is the commission of Christ to go and tell always reflected in your choices and actions?

_____

_____

_____

_____

_____

What difference could you make in the world around you should you always choose to act with this in mind?

_____

_____

_____

_____

_____

How does humility look when coupled with success?

_____

_____

_____

_____

_____

What is at the root of humility?

✎ _____

_____

_____

_____

Kingdom Extra

It takes courage and character to face adversity as Paul did. The only One who can prepare us to stand in the face of trouble is our heavenly Father working through His Son and Spirit.

If you're traveling down some tough roads now, or you know that just over the ridge trouble is waiting to ambush you, don't try to tackle it alone. Invite the God of peace to come alongside you as your travel companion. He may not deliver you from trouble's hands, but He will strengthen you to face adversity with Christ-like character and Spirit-directed power. Like Paul, you will be able to carry on, even in spite of any harm others may want to inflict on you.

Read John 16:33; 1 John 5:4–5; Romans 8:38–39.

Questions:

In the times of trouble you have faced in the past, how might the knowledge you have gained so far in this study enabled you to weather the storm more effectively?

✎ _____

_____

_____

_____

_____

Interdependent and Thankful

There isn't a human being—never has been and never will be—who hasn't drawn on someone's help at some time to do something. We come into this world with help, and we get through this world with help. We are dependent people, like it or not, acknowledge it or not.

The apostle Paul knew this. And to his credit, he not only accepted it but reveled in it. He loved the people he depended on. They were family to him, loved ones with incredible value because of who they were and what they did. He believed they deserved honor and respect, especially from fellow brothers and sisters in the faith. Christians, of all people, should embrace and support one another as family. Paul did that himself, and he expected other believers to do the same.

In the closing chapter of Romans, Paul spends the bulk of the space greeting various members of God's family in Rome (16:3–15) and offering greetings to all the Roman Christians on behalf of the believers who were with him, helping him with ministry (vv. 21–23). As we work through these closing verses, may we remember all those who have helped us along the way and renew our appreciation for them.

Read Philippians 1:3–11; 1 Corinthians 12:12–27.

Questions:

What feelings does the fact that you are dependent on others engender in you?

✎_____

_____

_____

_____

_____

How do you let those for whom you are thankful know of your gratitude?

✎_____

_____

_____

_____

_____

What reaction do you have to expressions of gratitude from others?

✎ _____

_____

_____

_____

_____

How can recognition of dependence and expression of gratitude strengthen the body of Christ?

✎ _____

_____

_____

_____

_____

What effect would this have on your closest relationships?

✎ _____

_____

_____

_____

_____

Record Your Thoughts

Some people refresh us and others challenge us. Take a look at the relationships in your life, and discern if they are to be in your life, and the reasons for thankfulness to God for what they bring.

✎ _____

_____

_____

_____

ADDITIONAL OBSERVATIONS

SESSION TWELVE

We Have the Words of Life

Kingdom Key—*Speak Blessing*

Numbers 6:22–27 "This is the way you shall bless the children of Israel." Say to them, 'The LORD bless you and keep you; the LORD make His face shine upon you, and be gracious to you; the LORD lift up His countenance upon you, and give you peace.' So they shall put My name on the children of Israel, and I will bless them."

This is a priestly blessing as dictated to Moses by God. Aaron was to speak this blessing over the children of Israel.

According to Revelation 1:4 we are kings and priests, so like Aaron, we have been given the power and authority to bless people in the name of Jesus Christ. Through blessing, the power of satan is crushed and God's power is released.

Read through the books that Paul wrote (Romans, 1 & 2 Corinthians, Galatians, Ephesians, Philippians, Colossians, 1 & 2 Thessalonians, the letters to Timothy, and Philemon). Note the times Paul speaks blessings and encouraging words.

Questions:

Why is it our responsibility to actively speak blessing into people's lives?

How do we extend God's goodness and His kingdom rule in people's lives when we bless them?

✎_____

_____

_____

_____

_____

Conclusion

Paul closes his Magna Carta of the Christian gospel with a fitting benediction—a doxology designed to review once more how much God has done and is doing for us and how faithful He is to His promises.

If you had been Paul writing the conclusion to this incredible letter, what would you have written? Draw upon what has meant the most to you in this study and put it in the form of praise to God and encouragement to other believers, as Paul did. Let these words stand as your summary of and refreshment in the gospel of Jesus Christ, our Lord and Savior forever. Amen.

Taking It All In

Review the Kingdom Keys that we have studied throughout this study of Kingdom Living. Write in your own words what each one means to you as you step forward into life beyond limits—life in the kingdom of God.

   1. **Christ Is Our Righteousness**

✎_____

_____

_____

_____

_____

2. All Have Sinned

_____

_____

_____

_____

_____

3. We Are Reconciled to God

_____

_____

_____

_____

_____

4. We Are Justified by Faith

_____

_____

_____

_____

_____

5. We Are Delivered

_____

_____

_____

_____

_____

6. We Choose Our Master

_____

_____

_____

_____

_____

7. We Are Heirs

_____
_____
_____
_____
_____

8. God Is Faithful to His Word

_____
_____
_____
_____
_____

9. We Are Being Changed

_____
_____
_____
_____
_____

10. We Are Aliens

_____
_____
_____
_____

11. Maintain a Sure Focus

_____
_____
_____
_____
_____

12. Speak Blessing

_____
_____
_____
_____
_____

We are citizens of a new kingdom; one with precepts, laws, social mores and rules of conduct. It is totally different from the kingdom of this world, and it takes time and determination to learn to walk in this new cosmology. It is a new socialization process.

God has showered upon His people blessings of infinite worth. He has sent His Son to be our righteousness, taken away the penalty for our sin, opened wide the doors of His kingdom, returned us to an effectively sinless state, cleansed us, healed us and made us whole, given us the honor of serving Him, given all He is as an inheritance, remained faithful regardless of our actions and attitudes, transformed us, created new beings, given us purpose and meaning and the ability to pass life and blessings to others.

Oh what a mighty God we serve! May we never cease to praise Him for all He has done, all He is presently doing and for the faithful promises we find in Him. God has truly provided abundantly for all of life.

ADDITIONAL OBSERVATIONS